THIS BOOK BELONGS TO:

Copyright 2021
Artist: Annamarie J. Lopez
All images are intellectual property of the artist and may not be reproduced.
www.witch-haunt.com

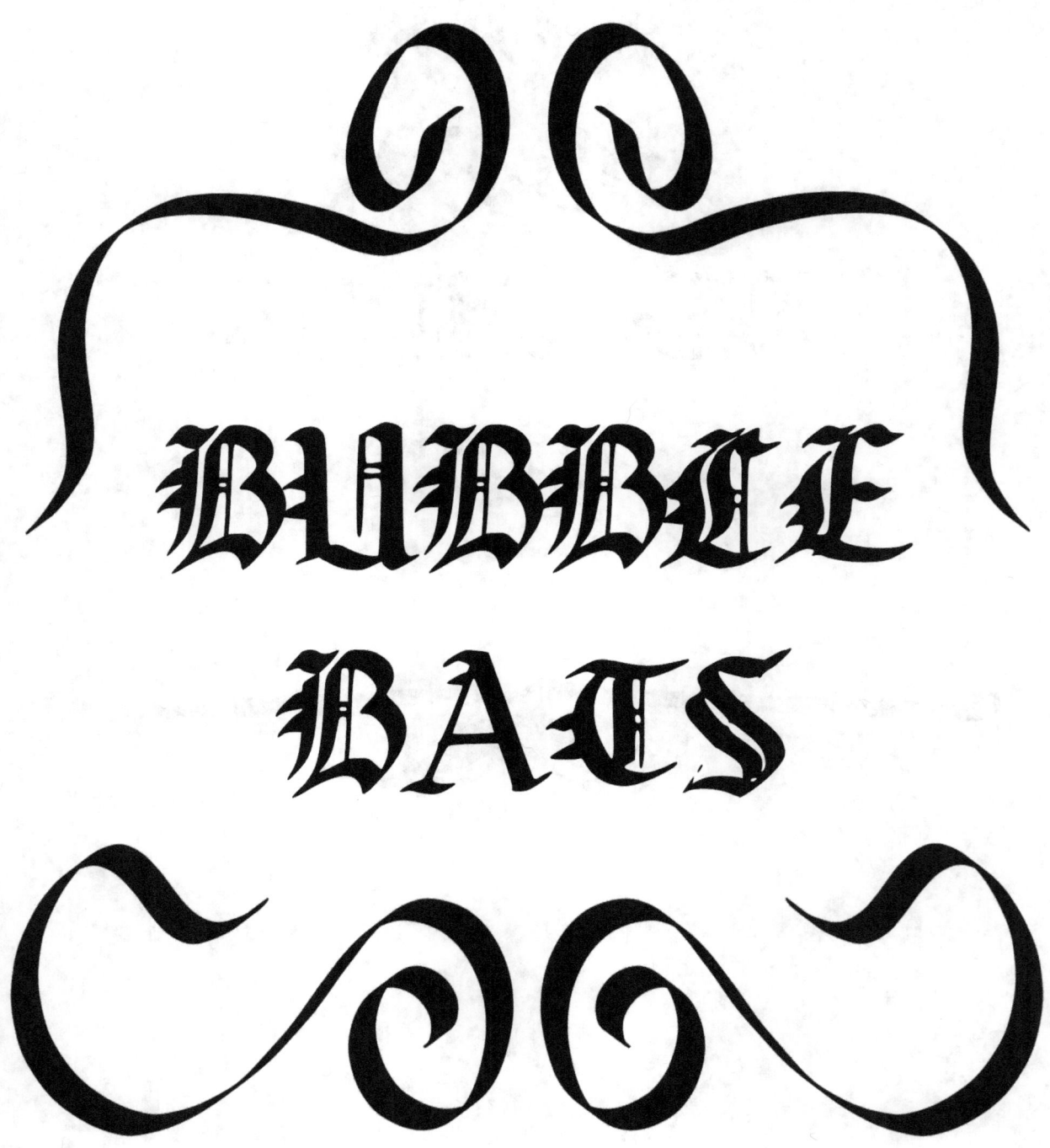

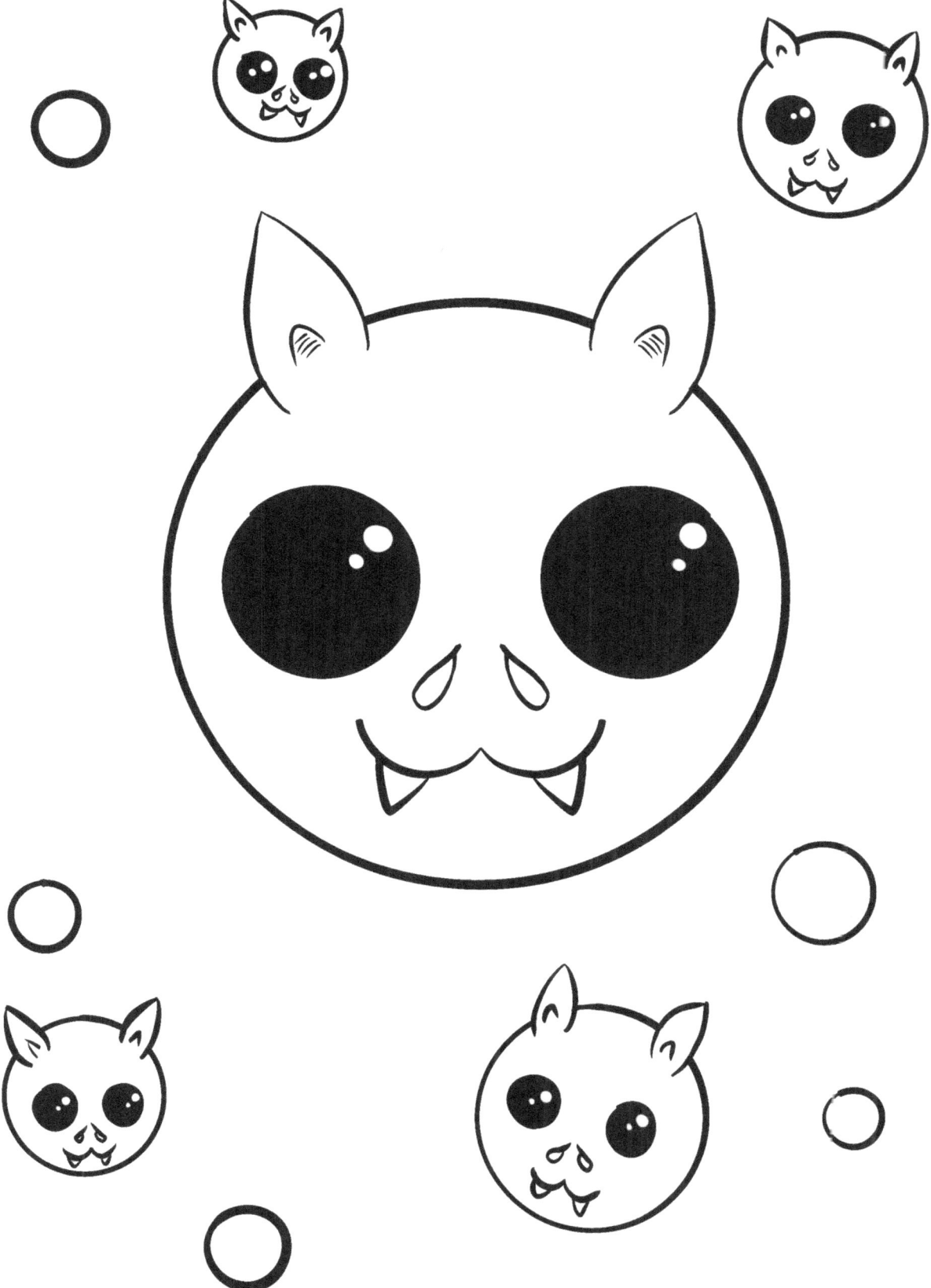

MOON PHASE PATTERNS

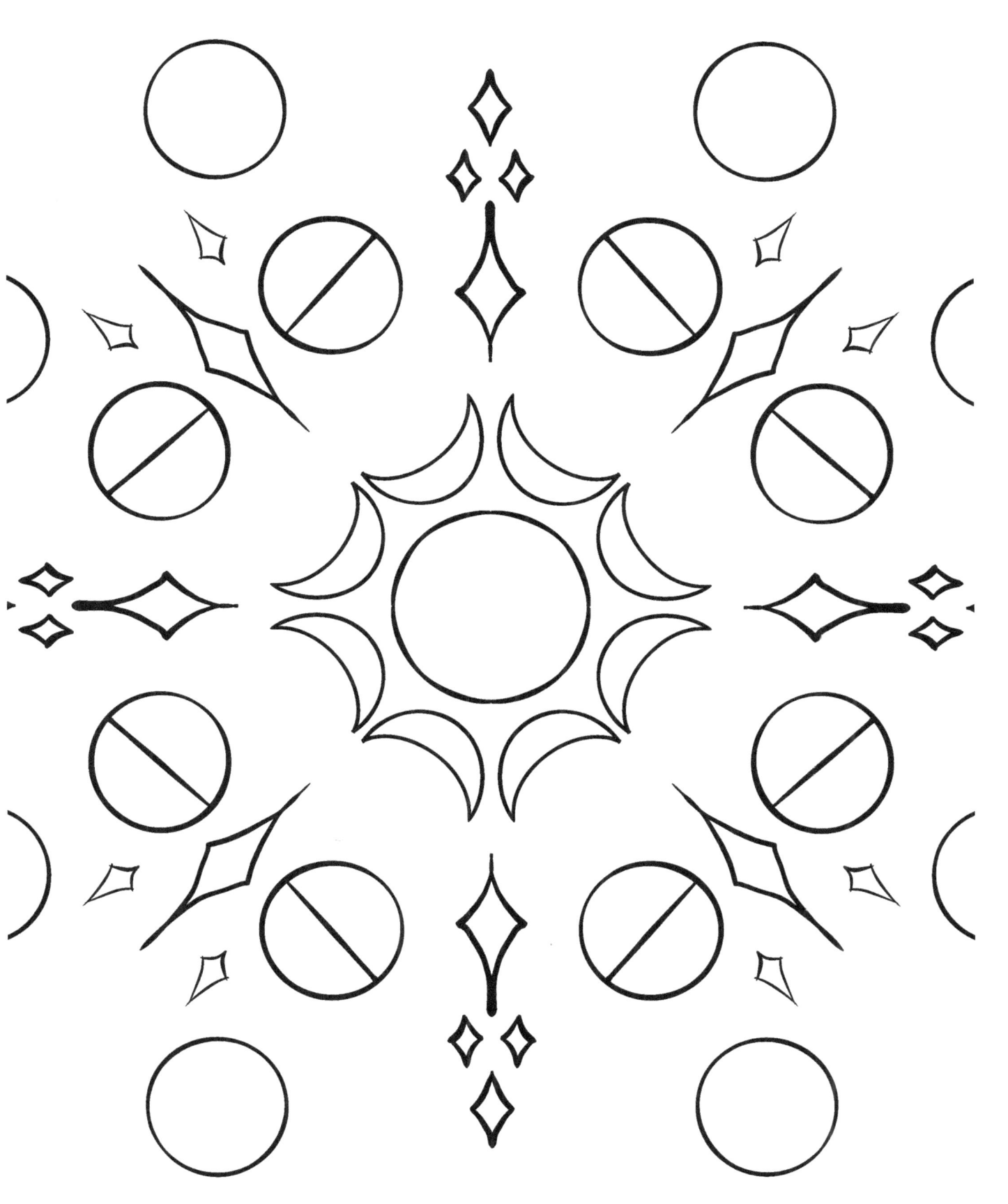

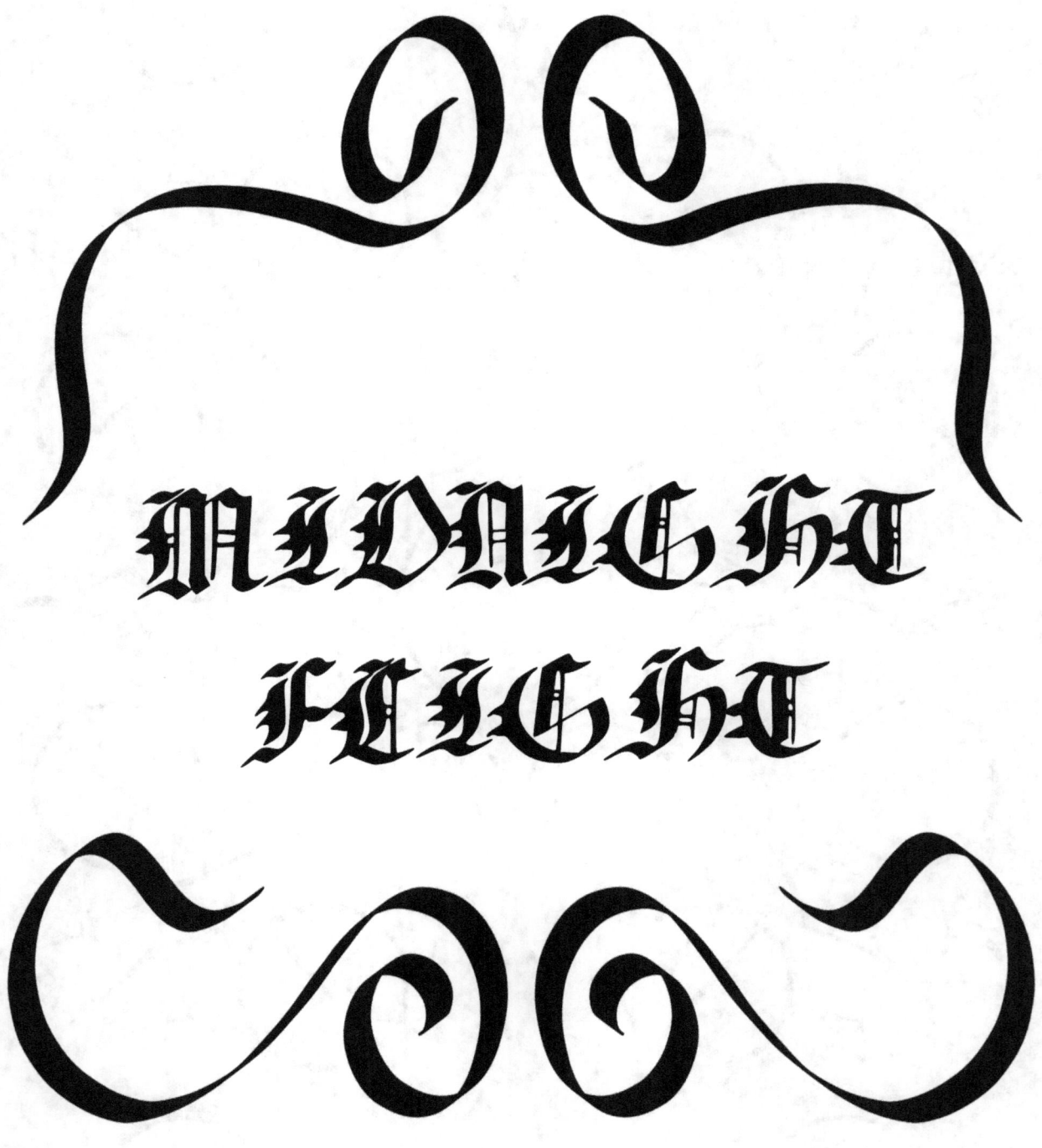

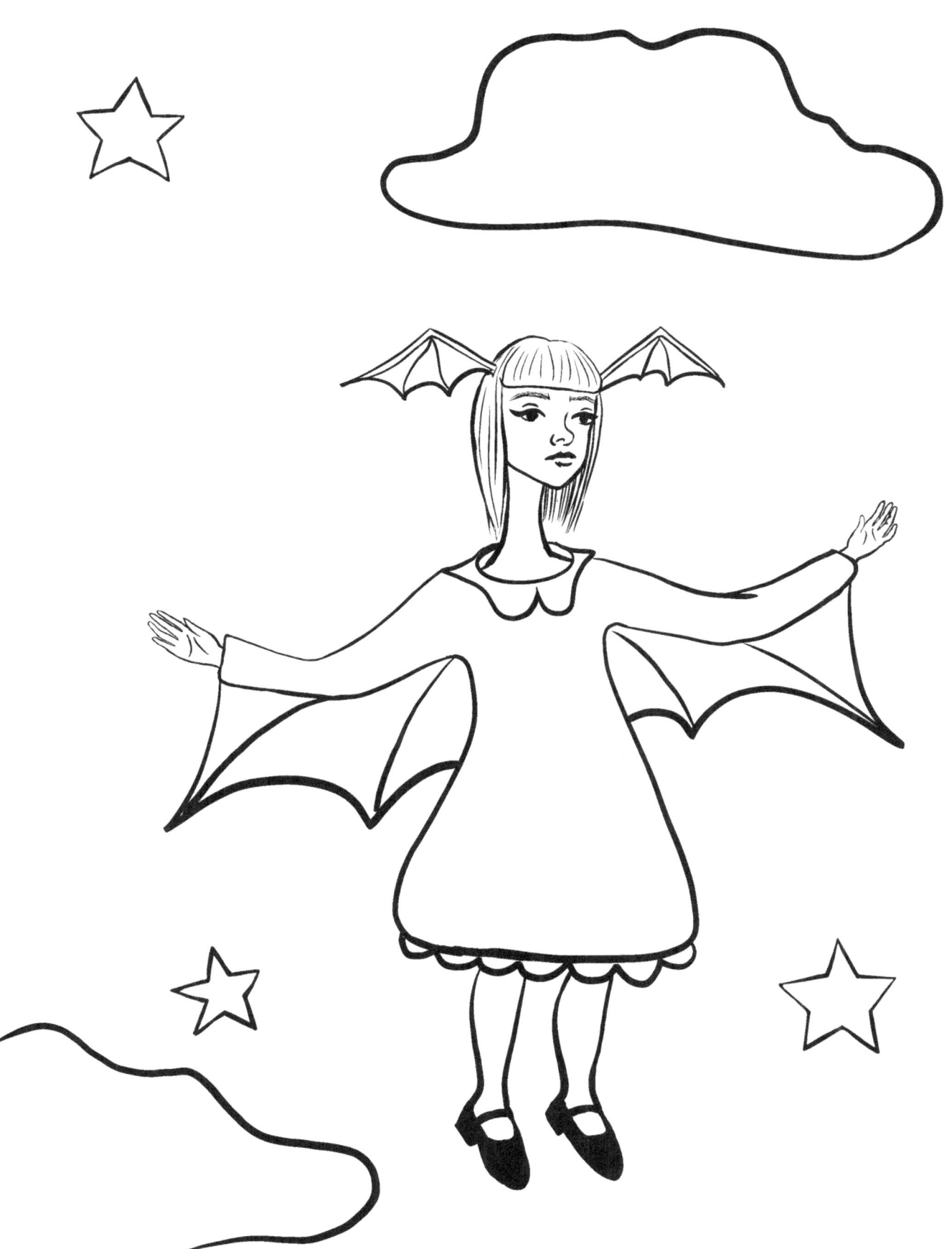

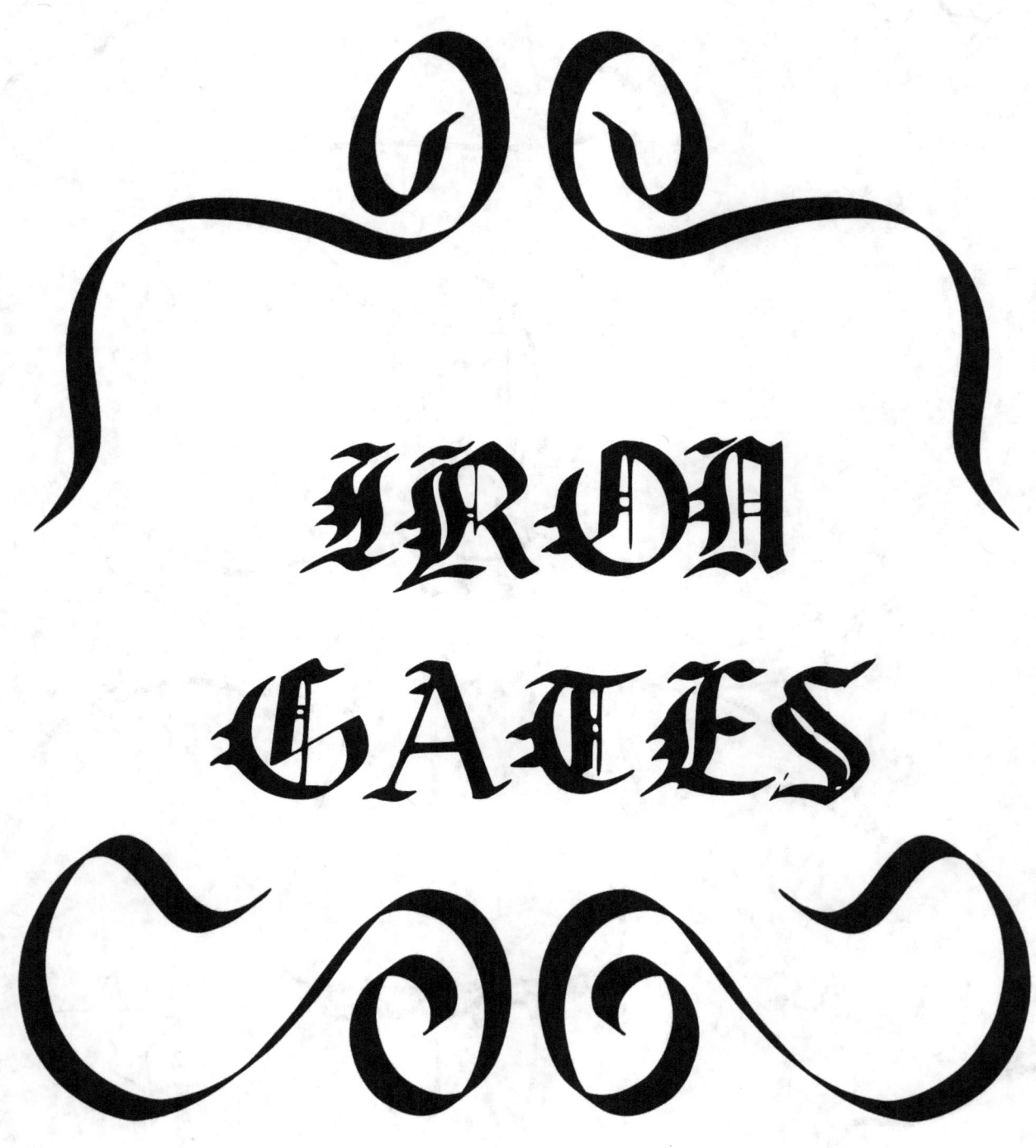

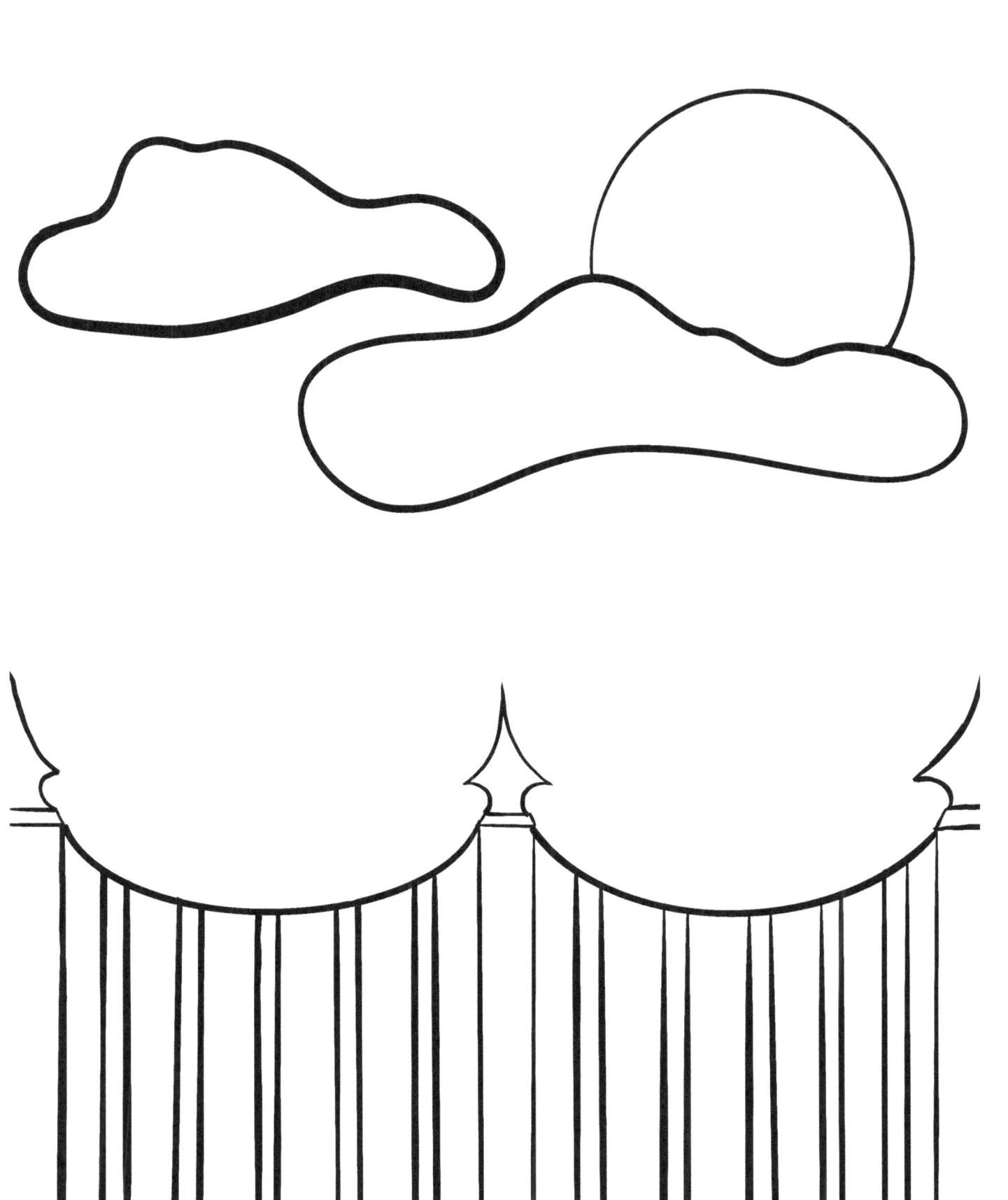

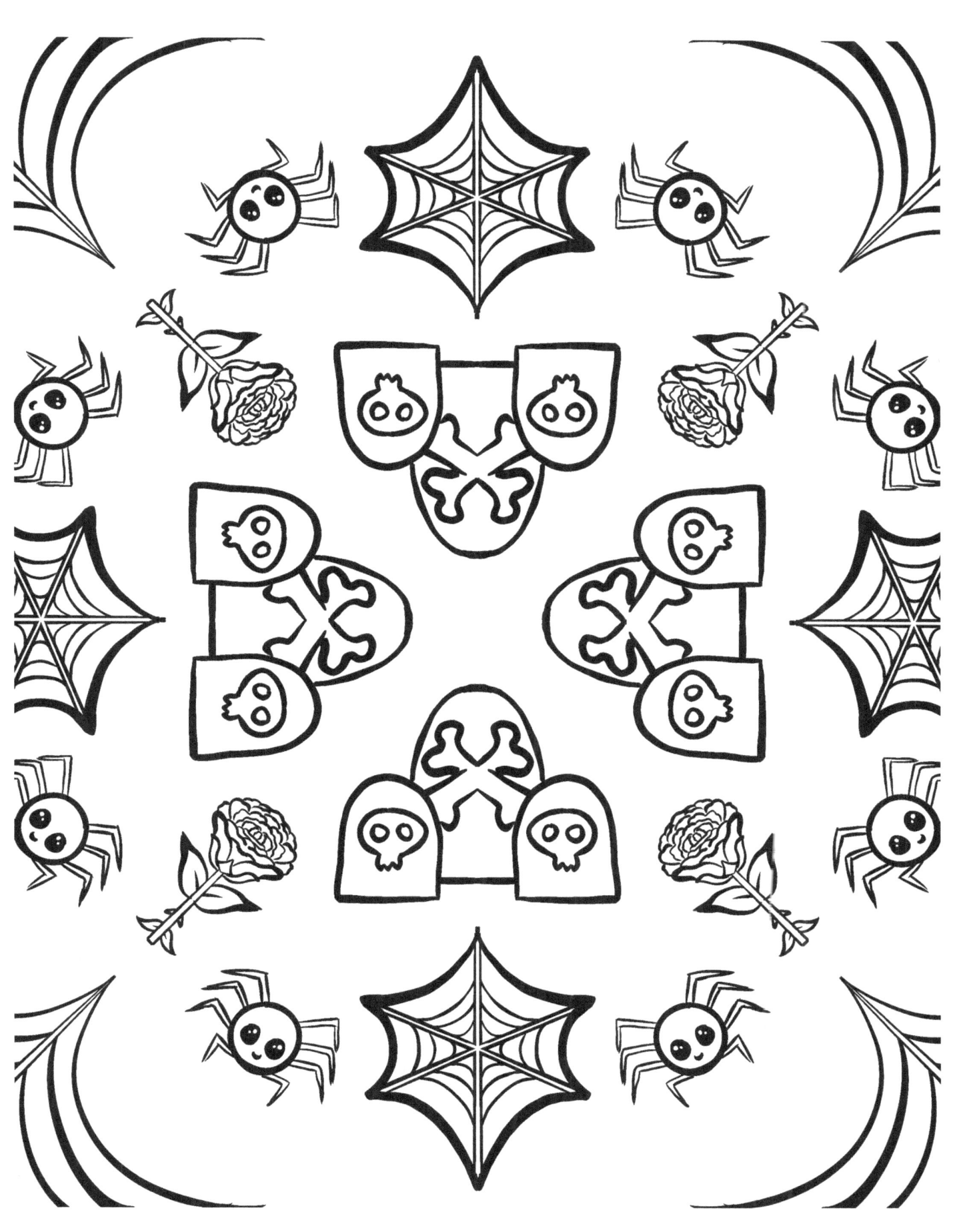

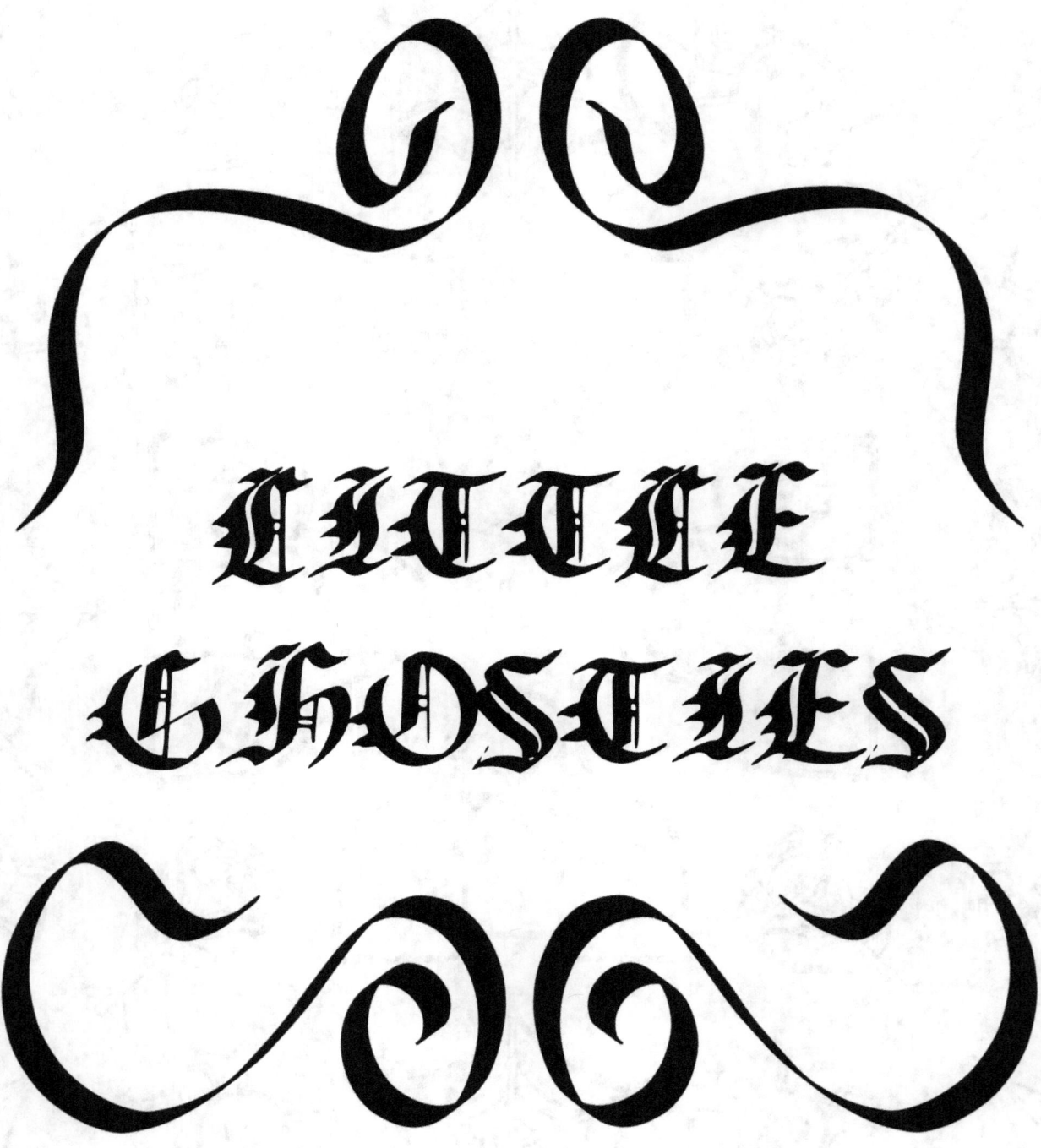

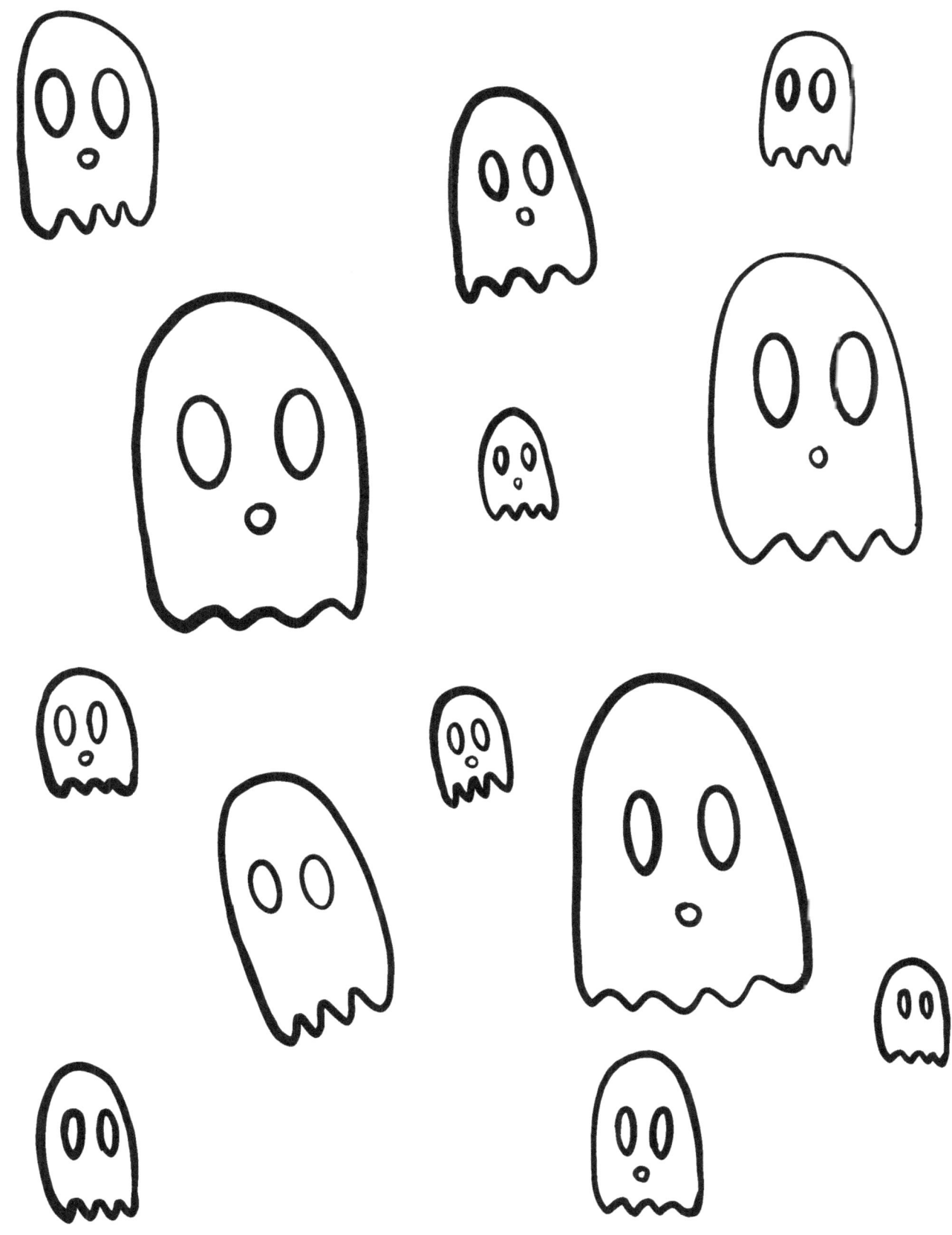

KITTY AND MOON PHASES

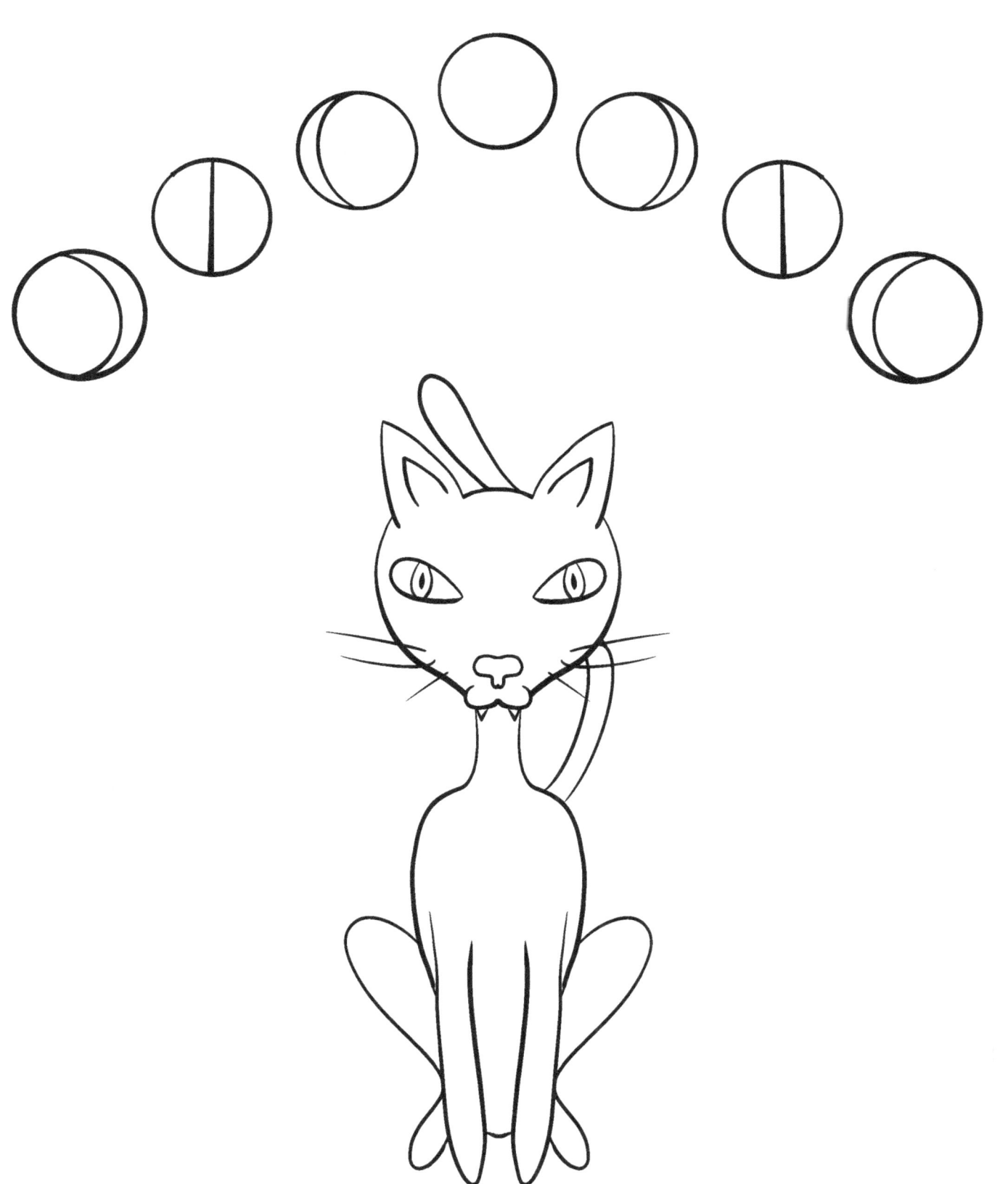

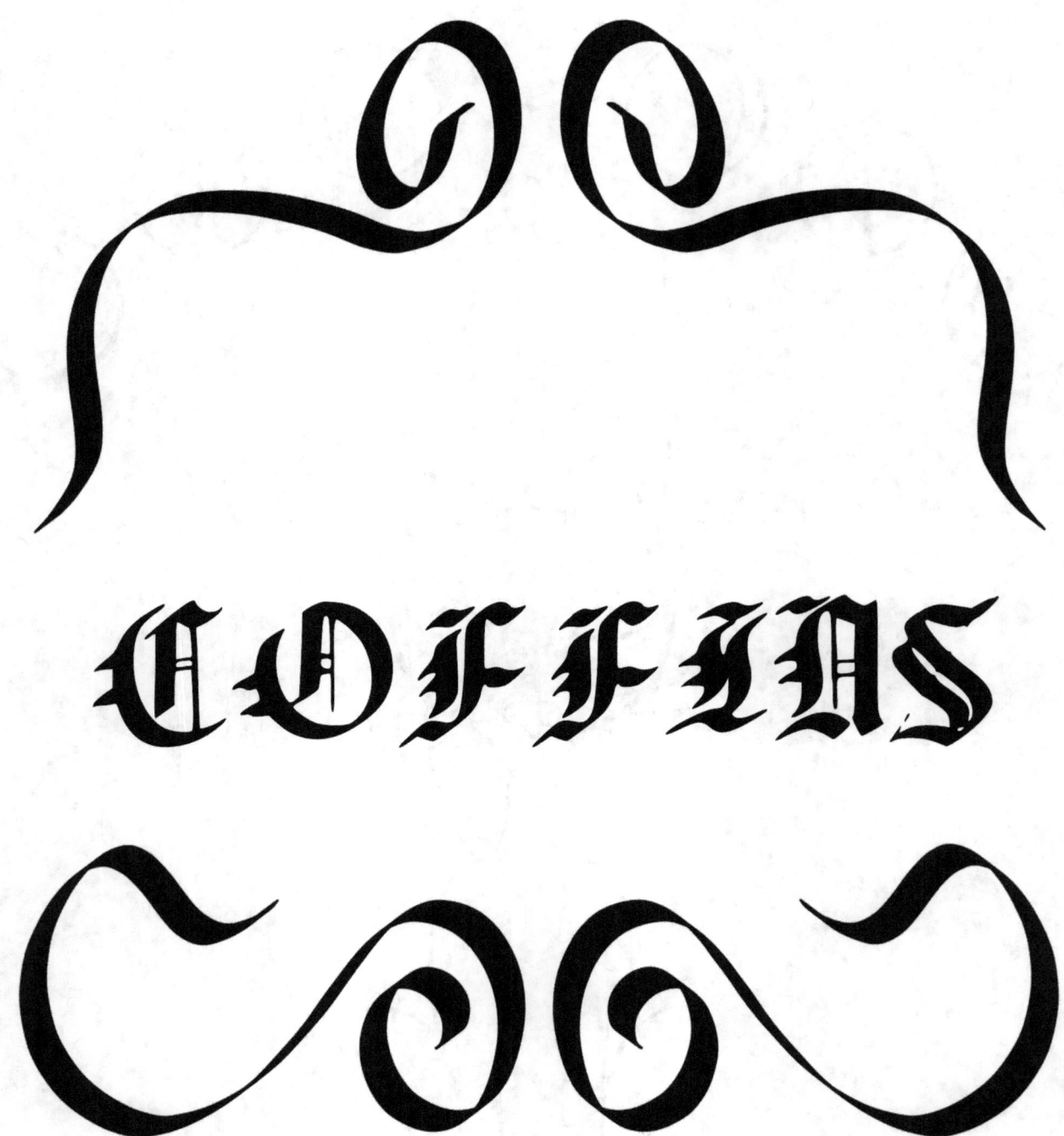

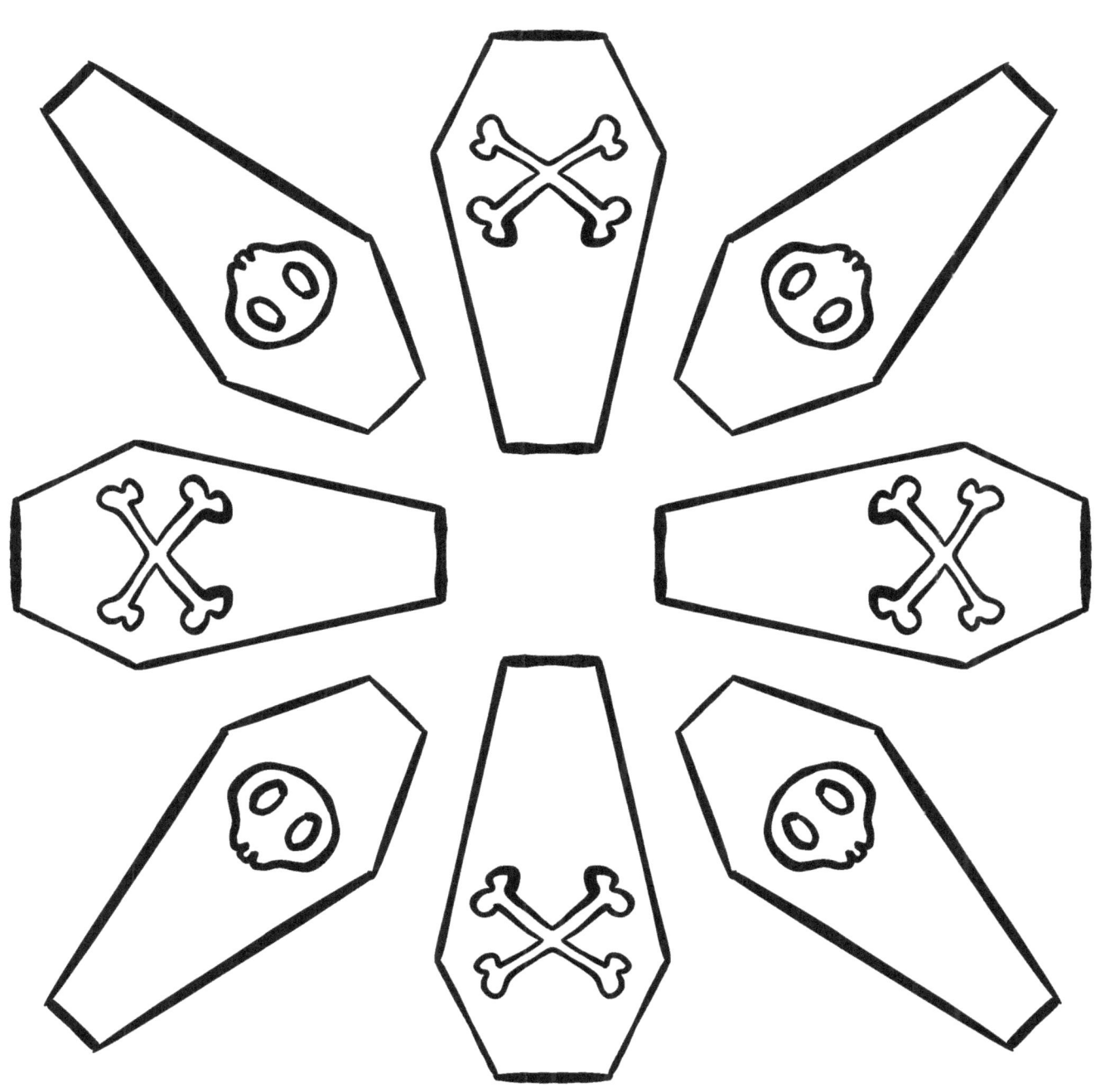

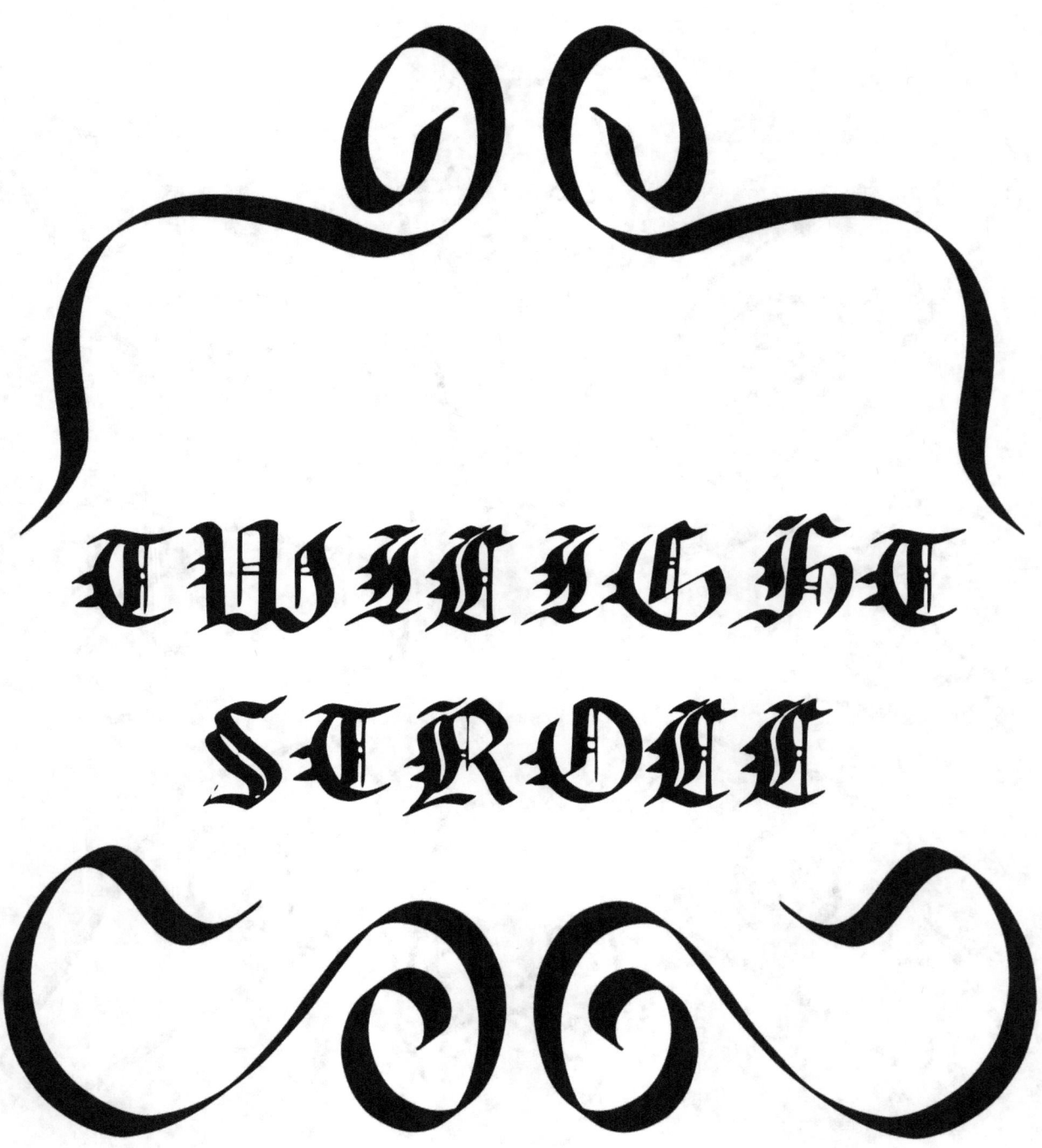

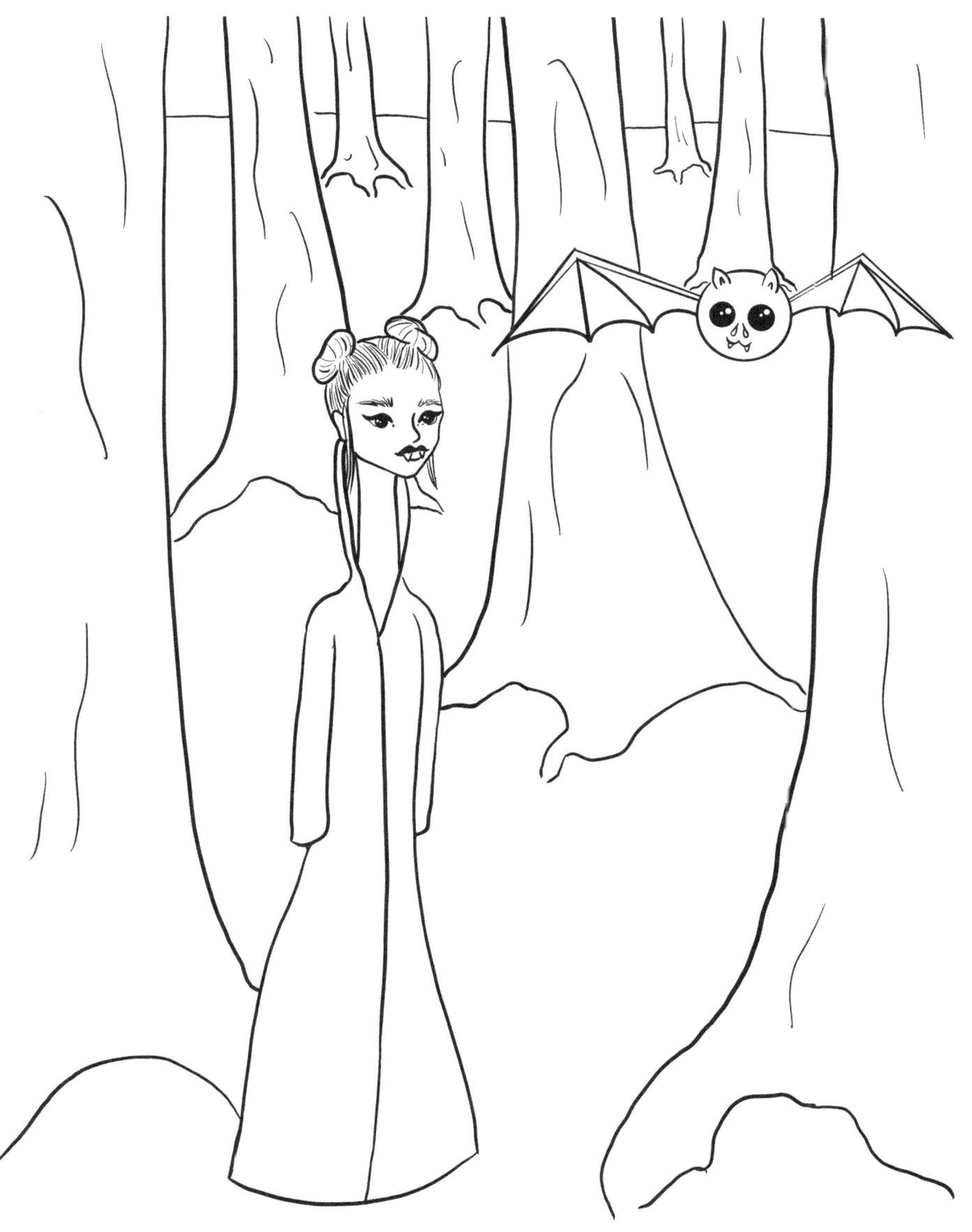

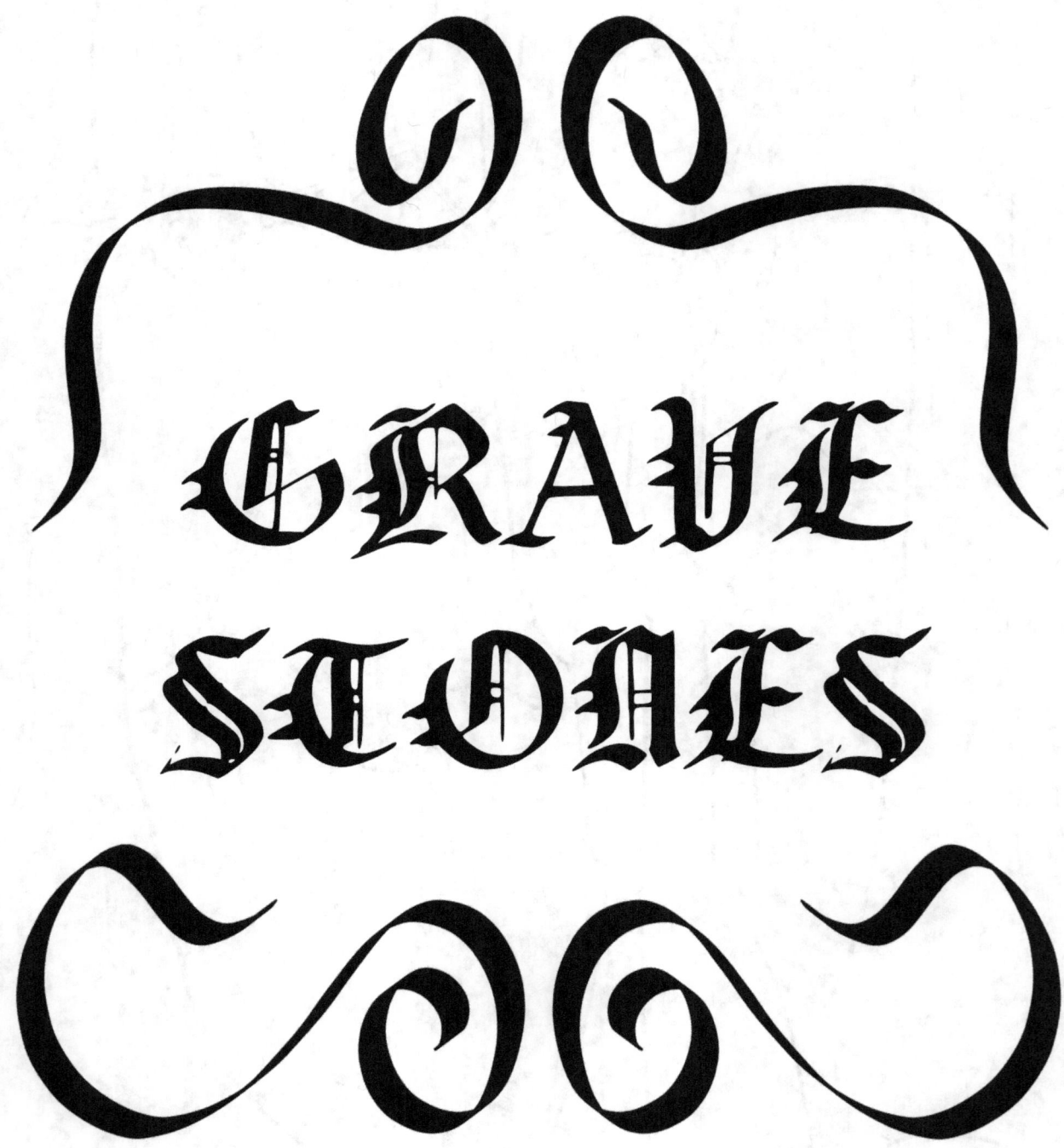

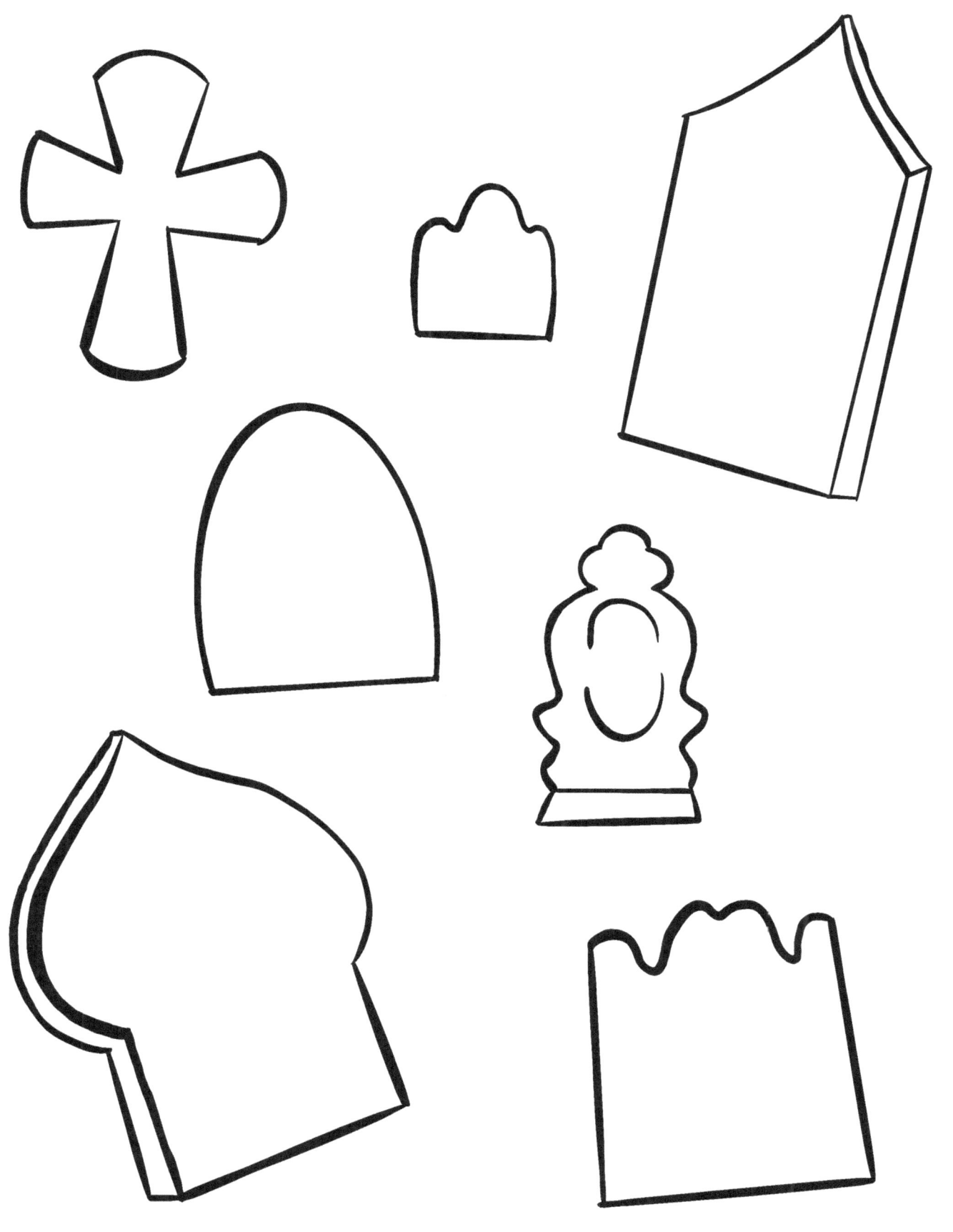

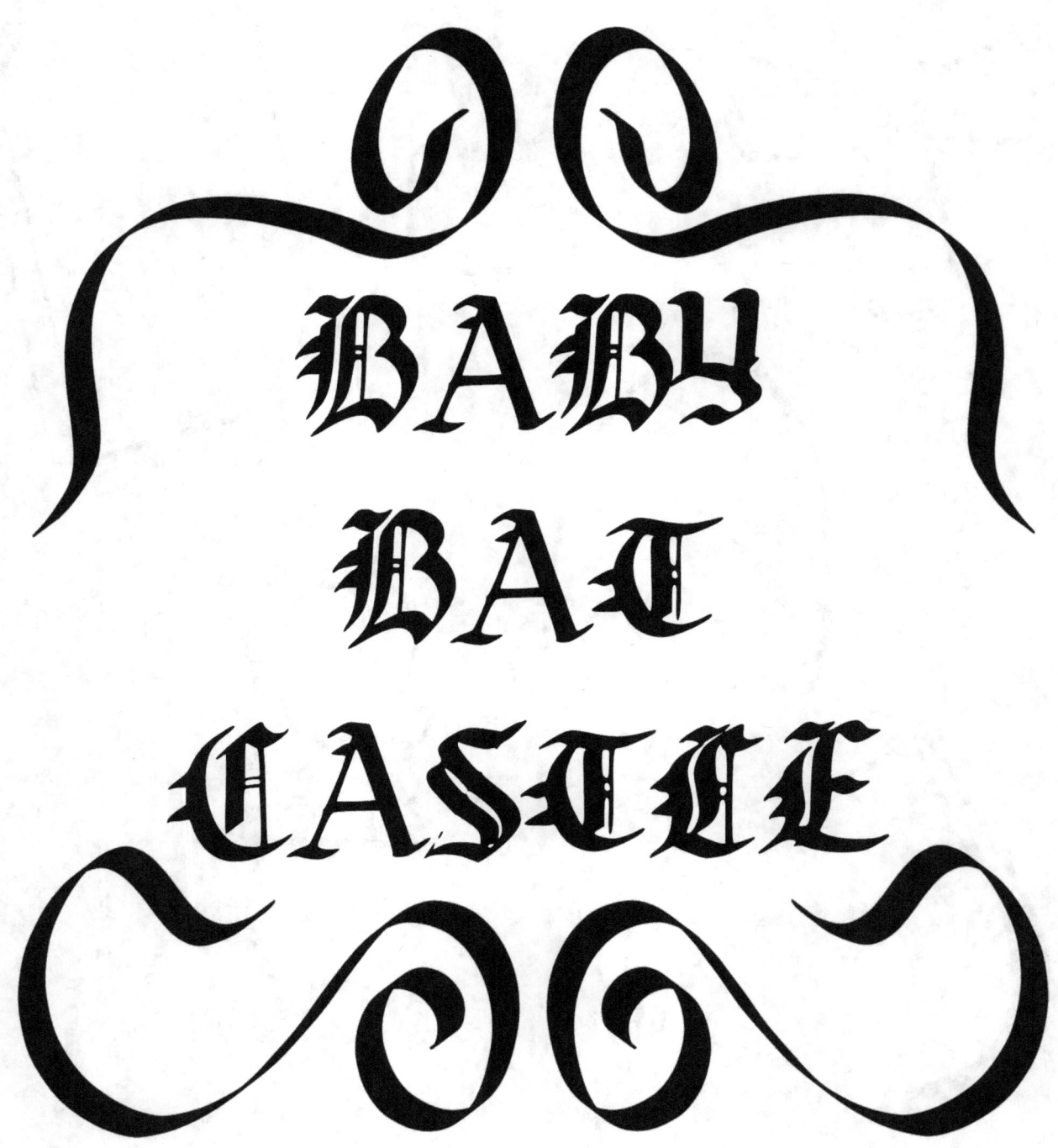

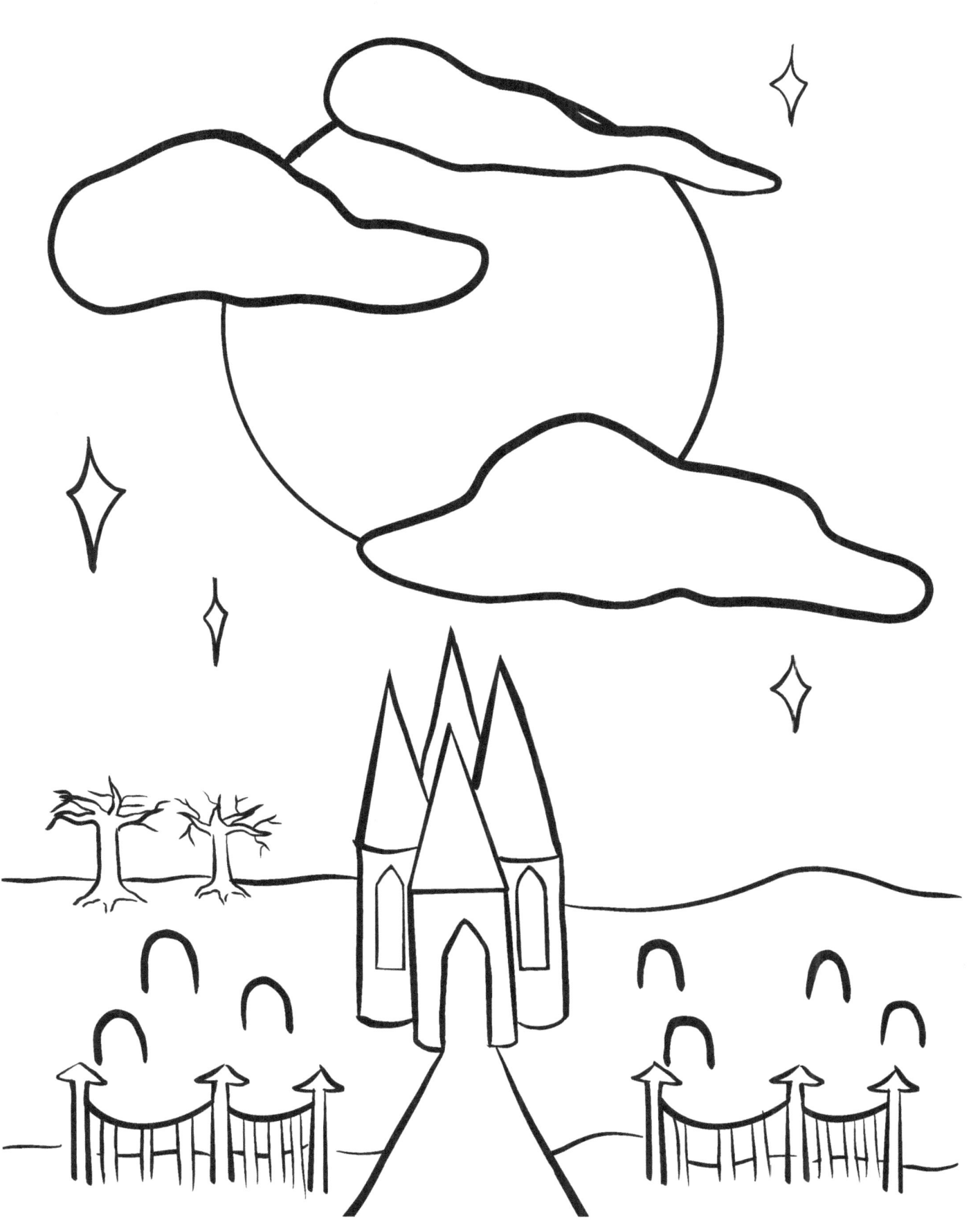

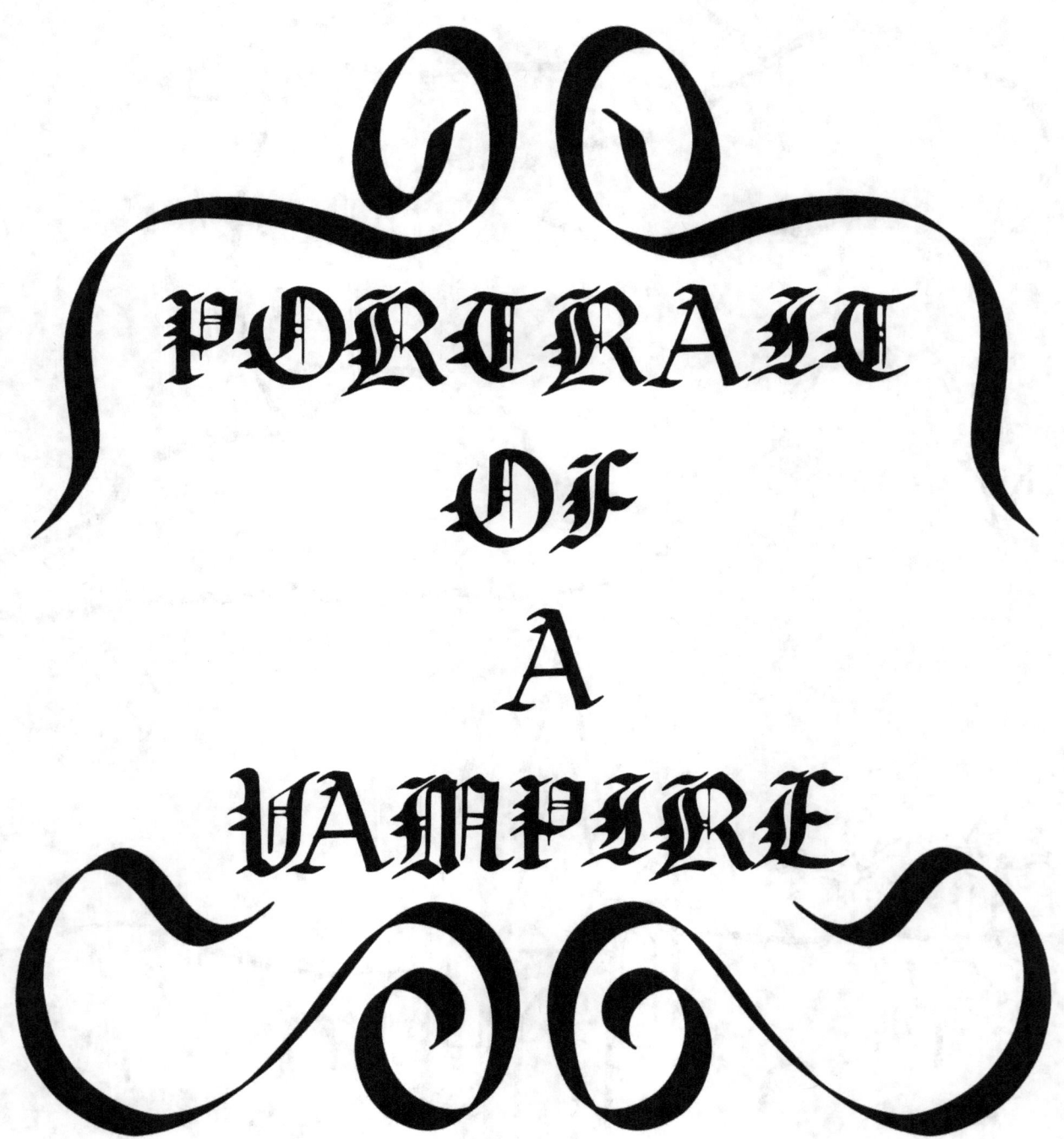

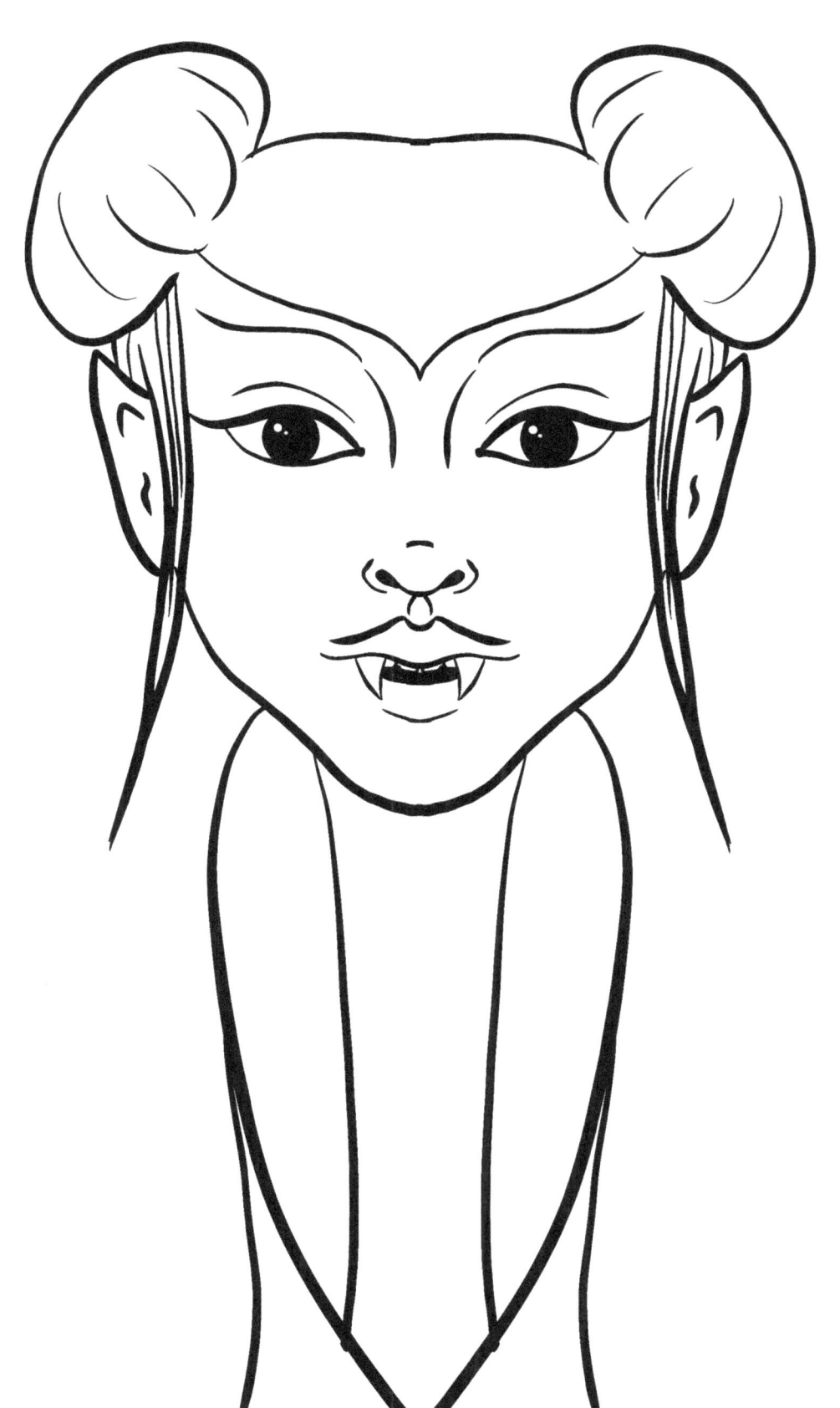

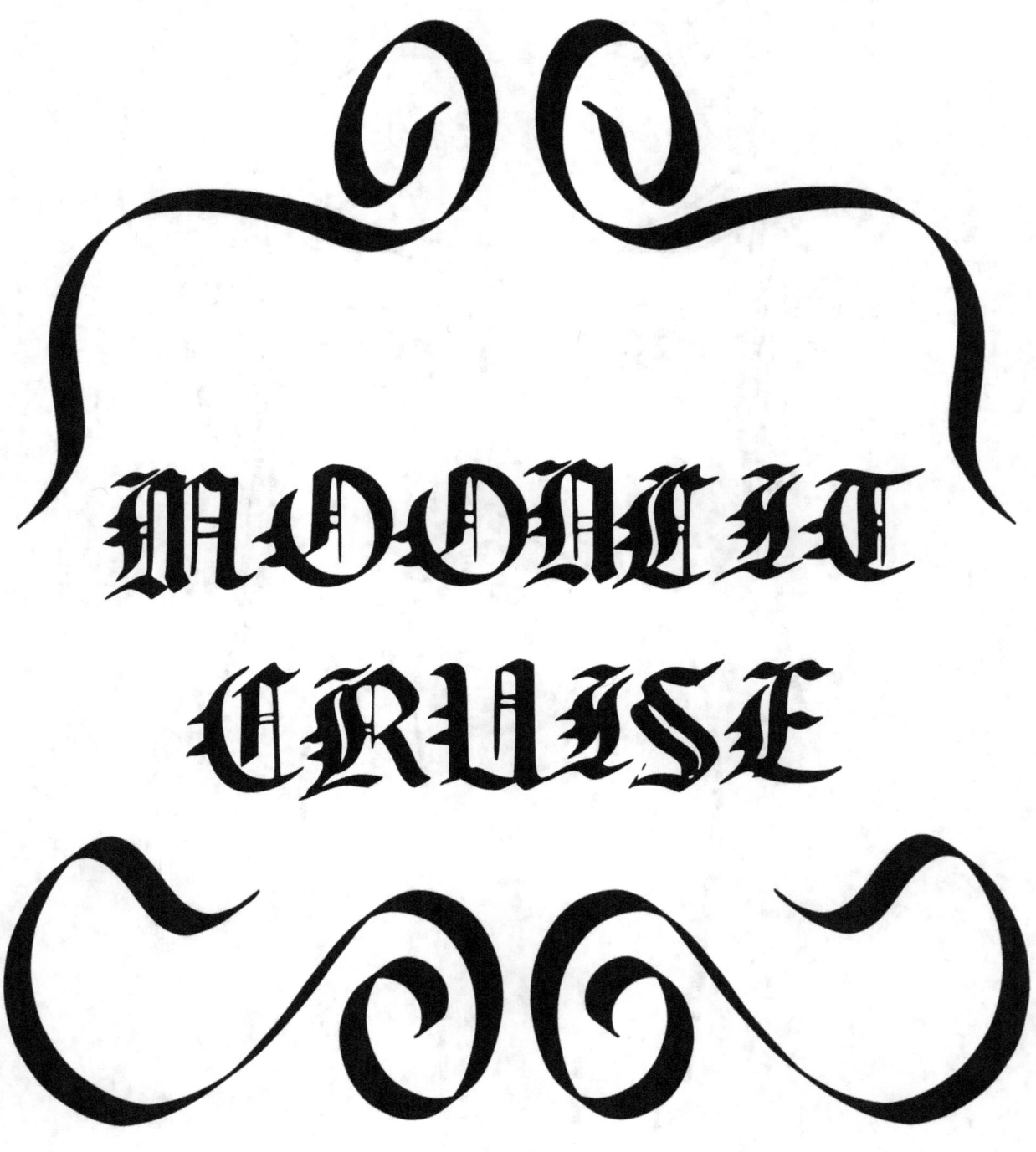

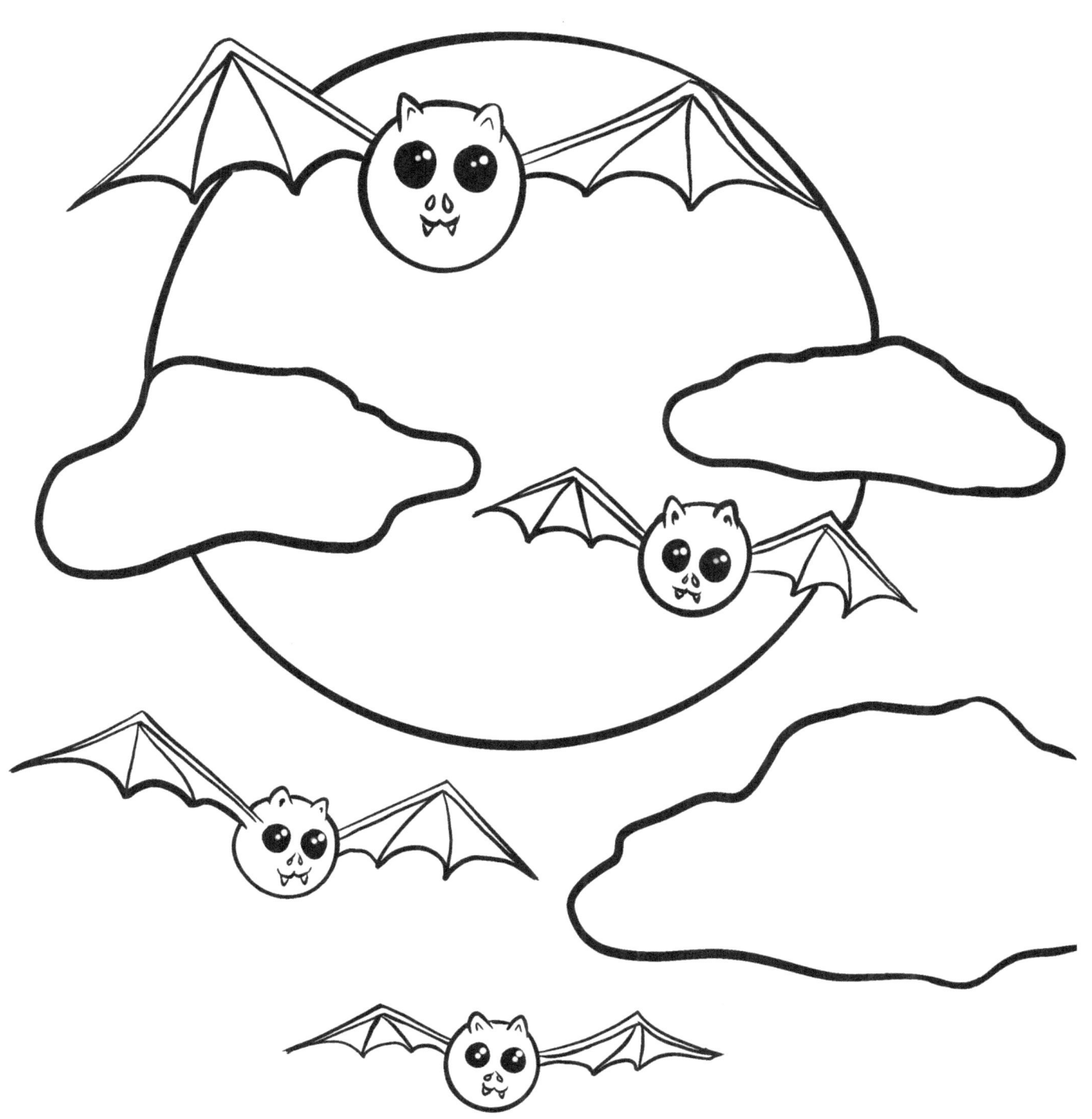

SPIDER PATTERN

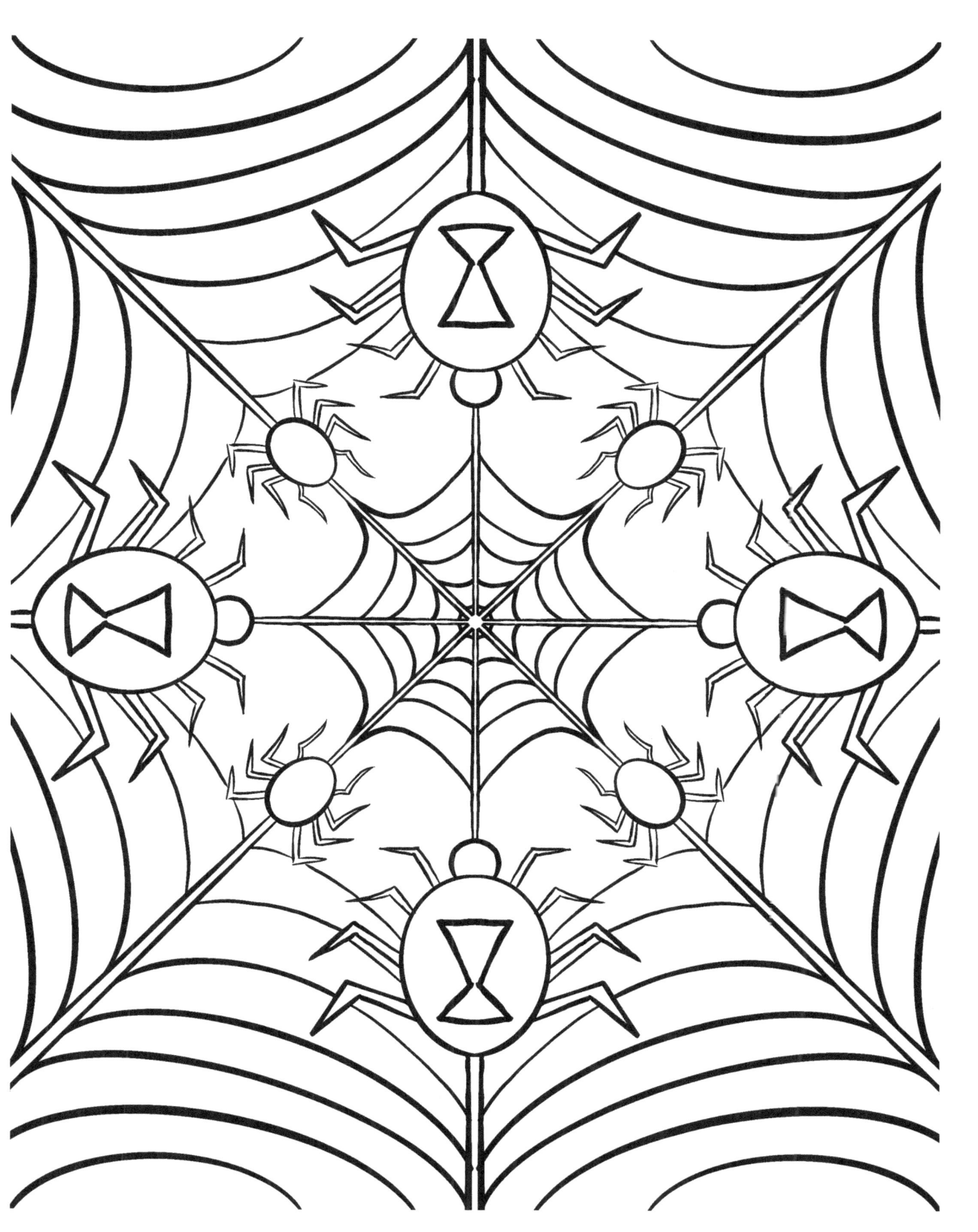

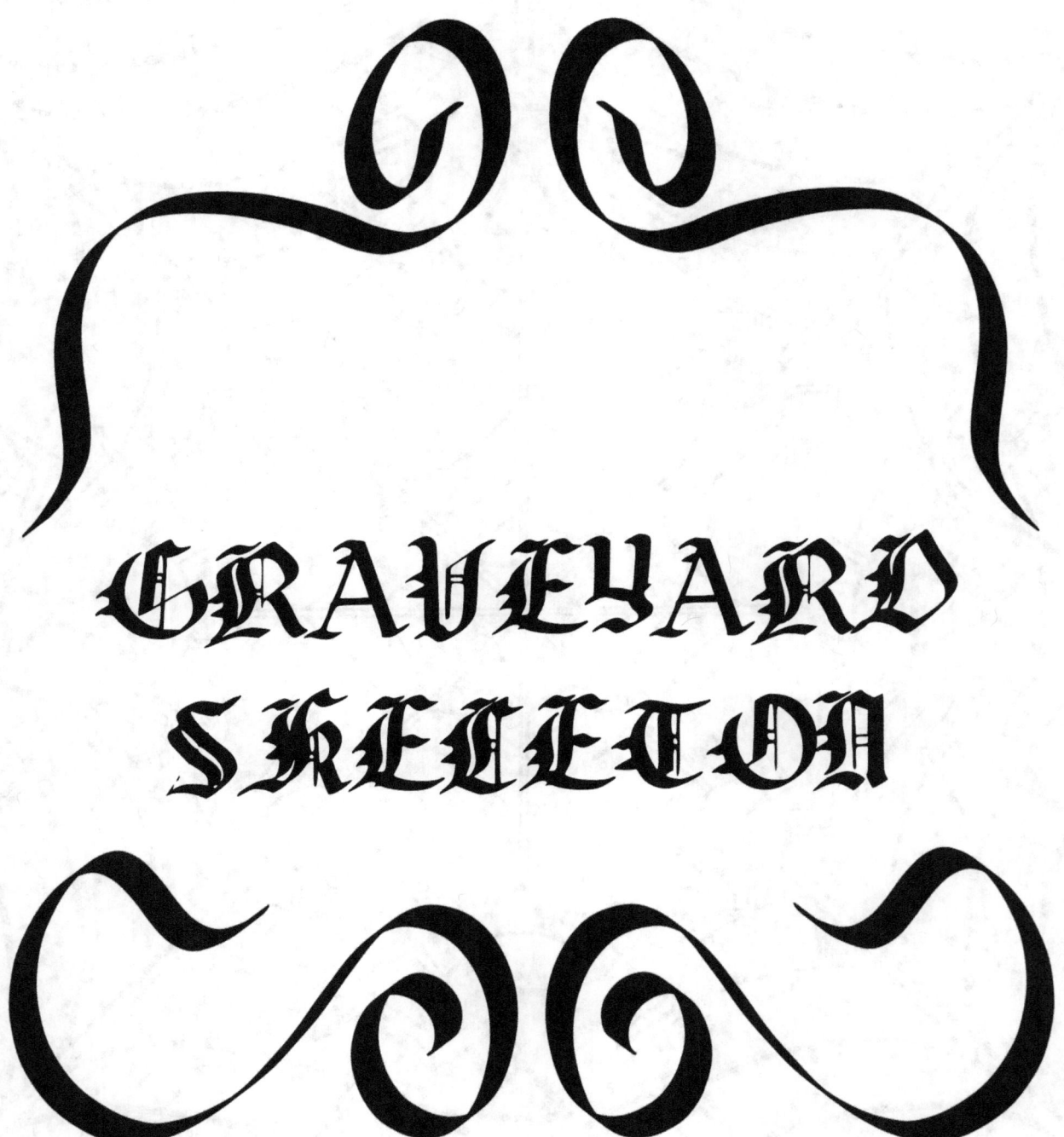

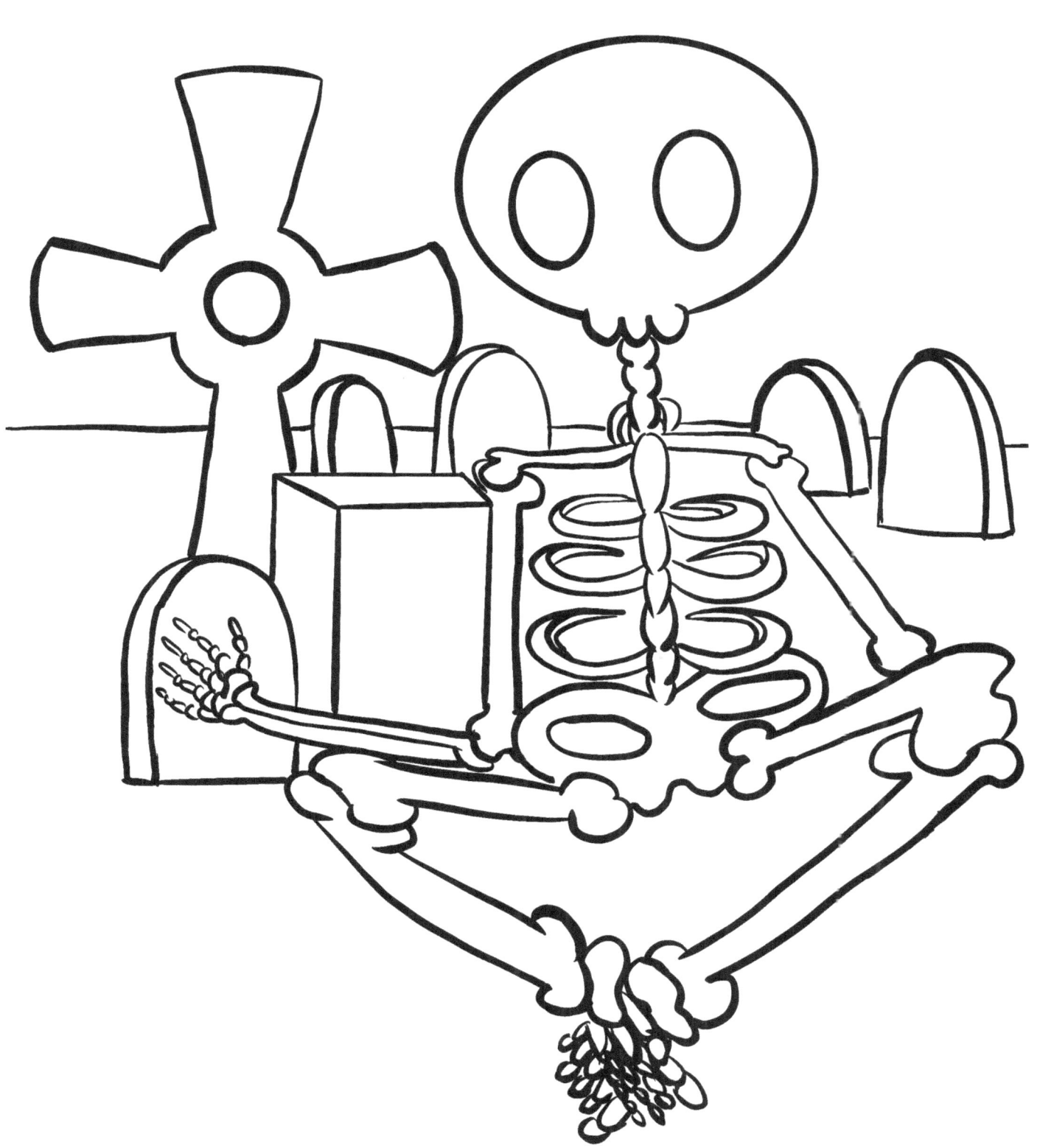

GHOST PATTERN

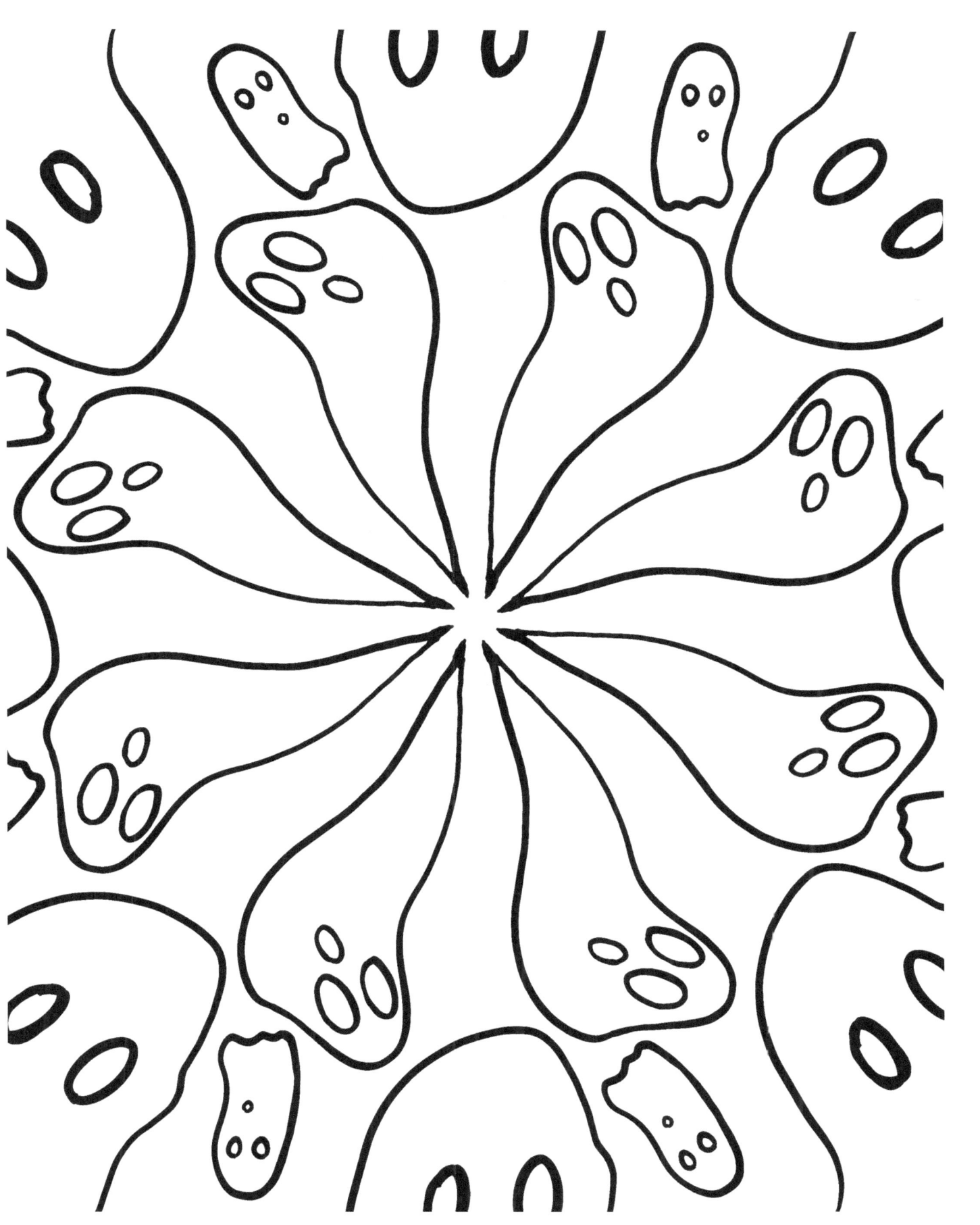

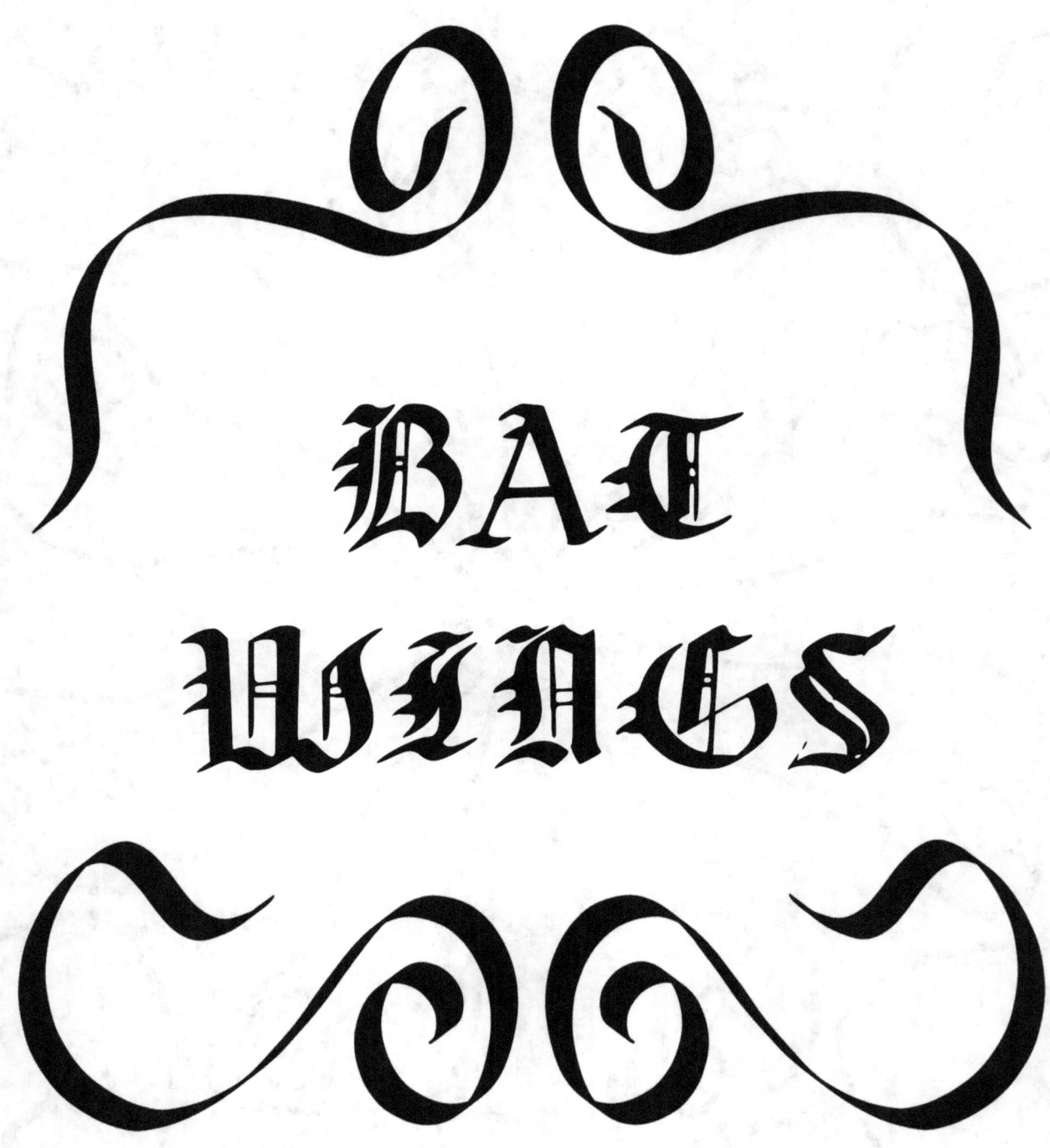

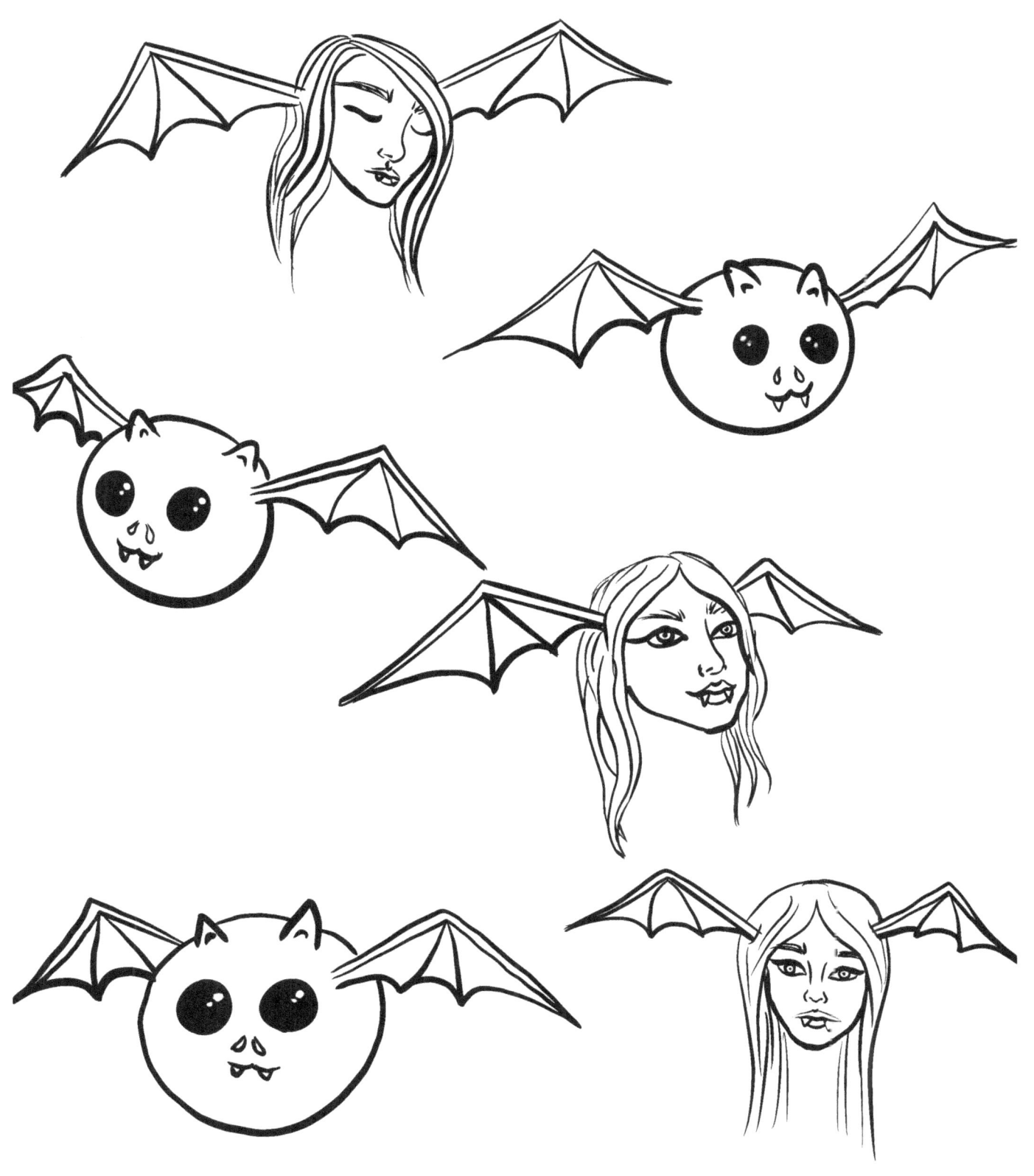

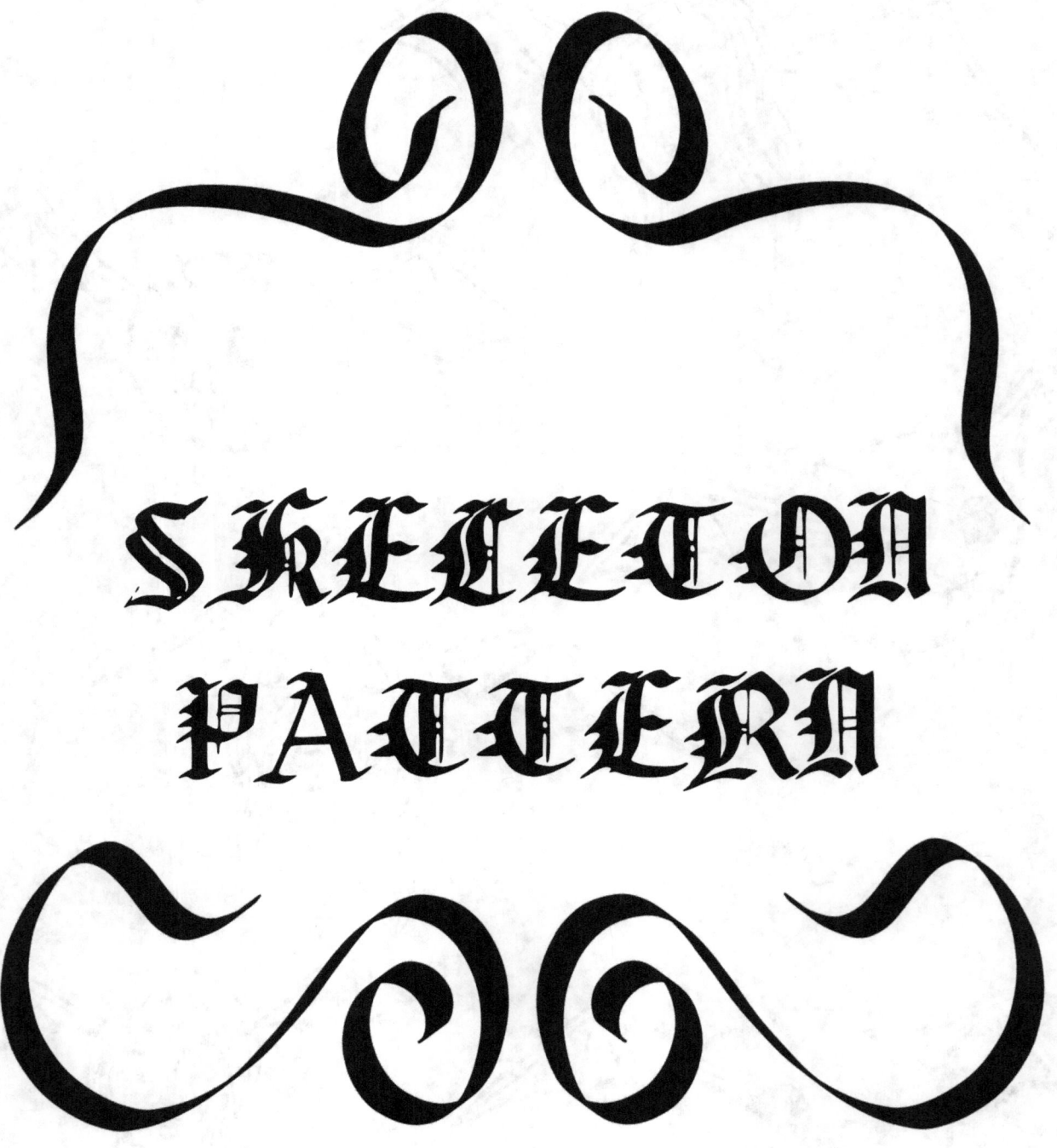

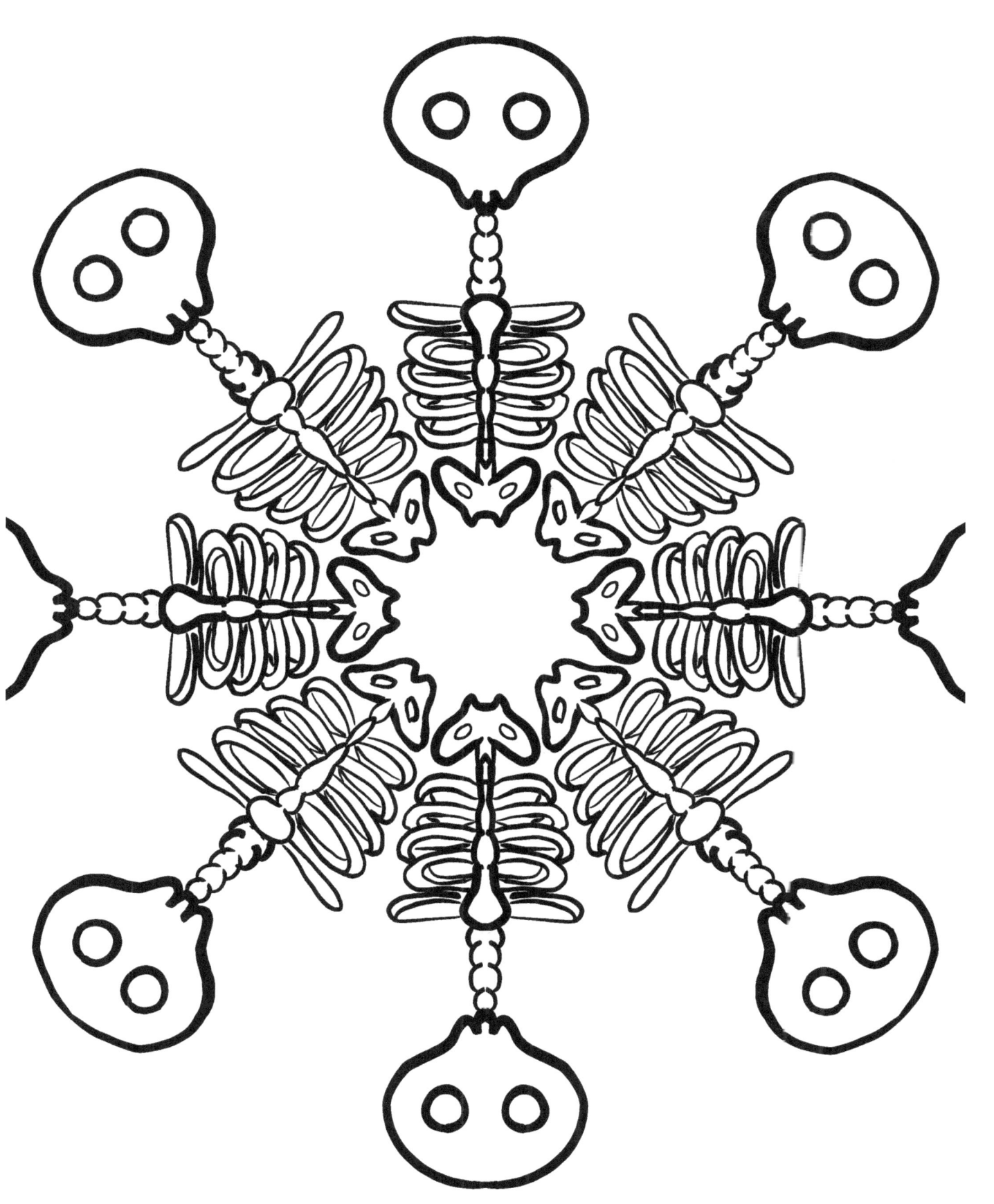

LITTLE SPIDERS

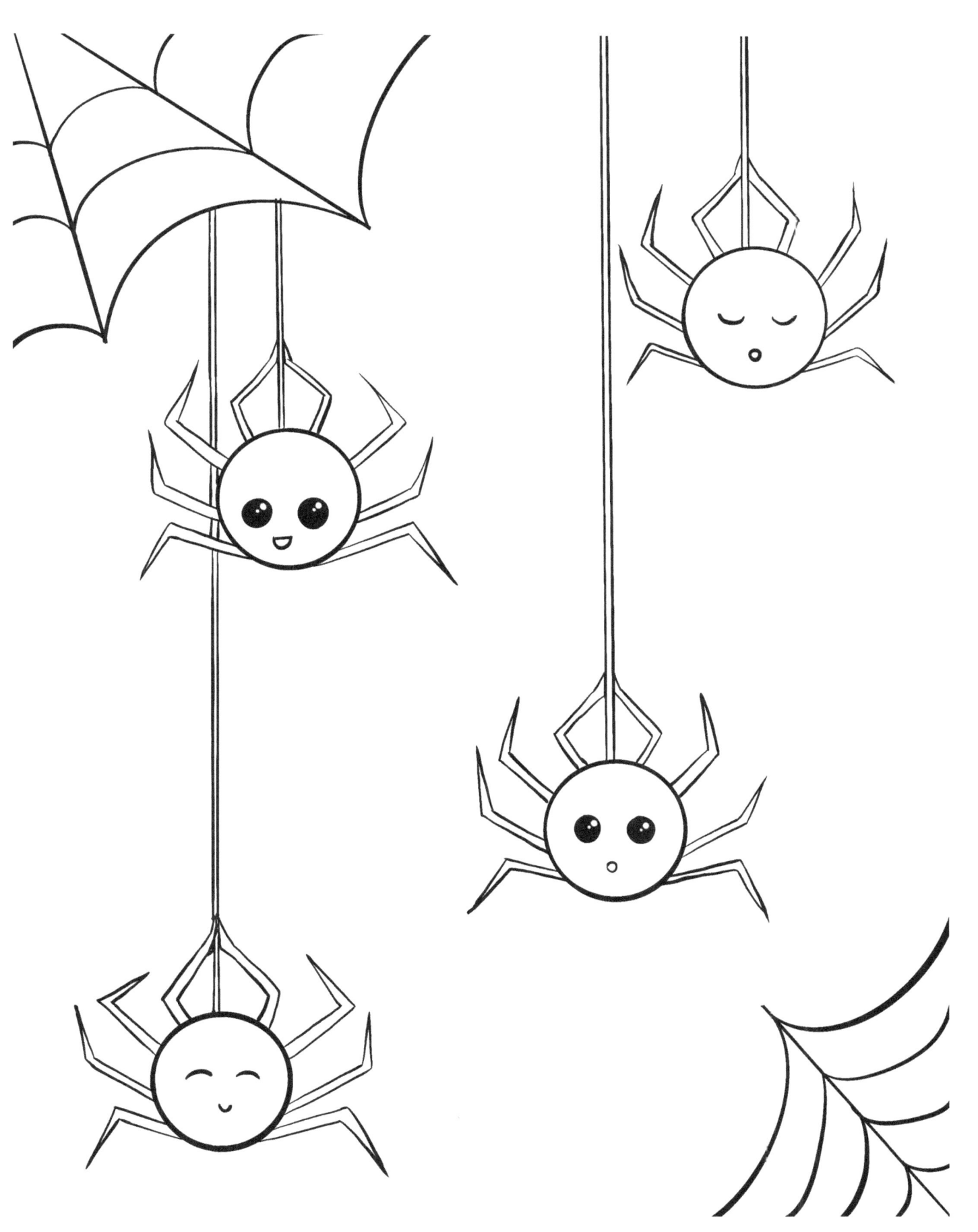

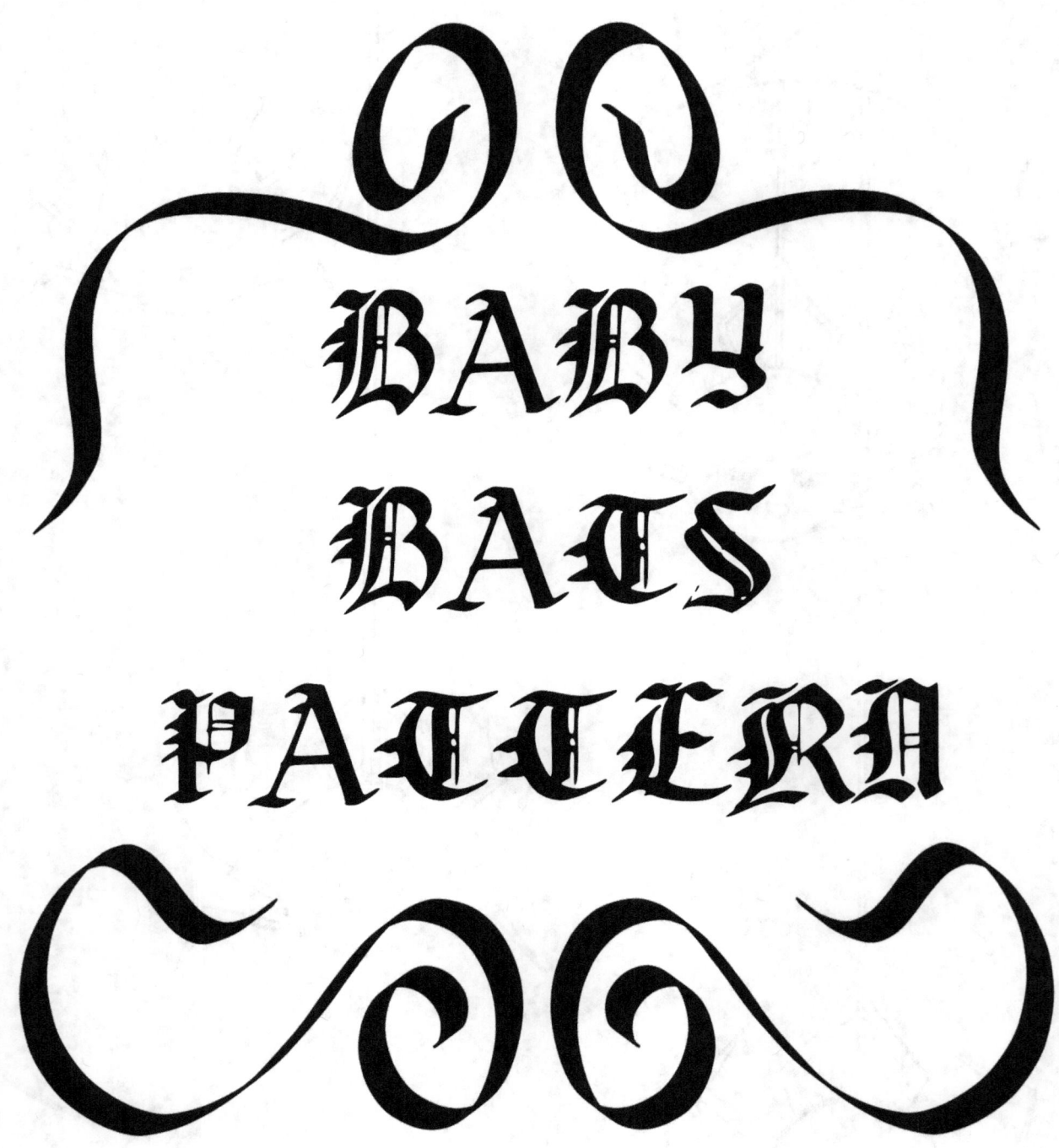

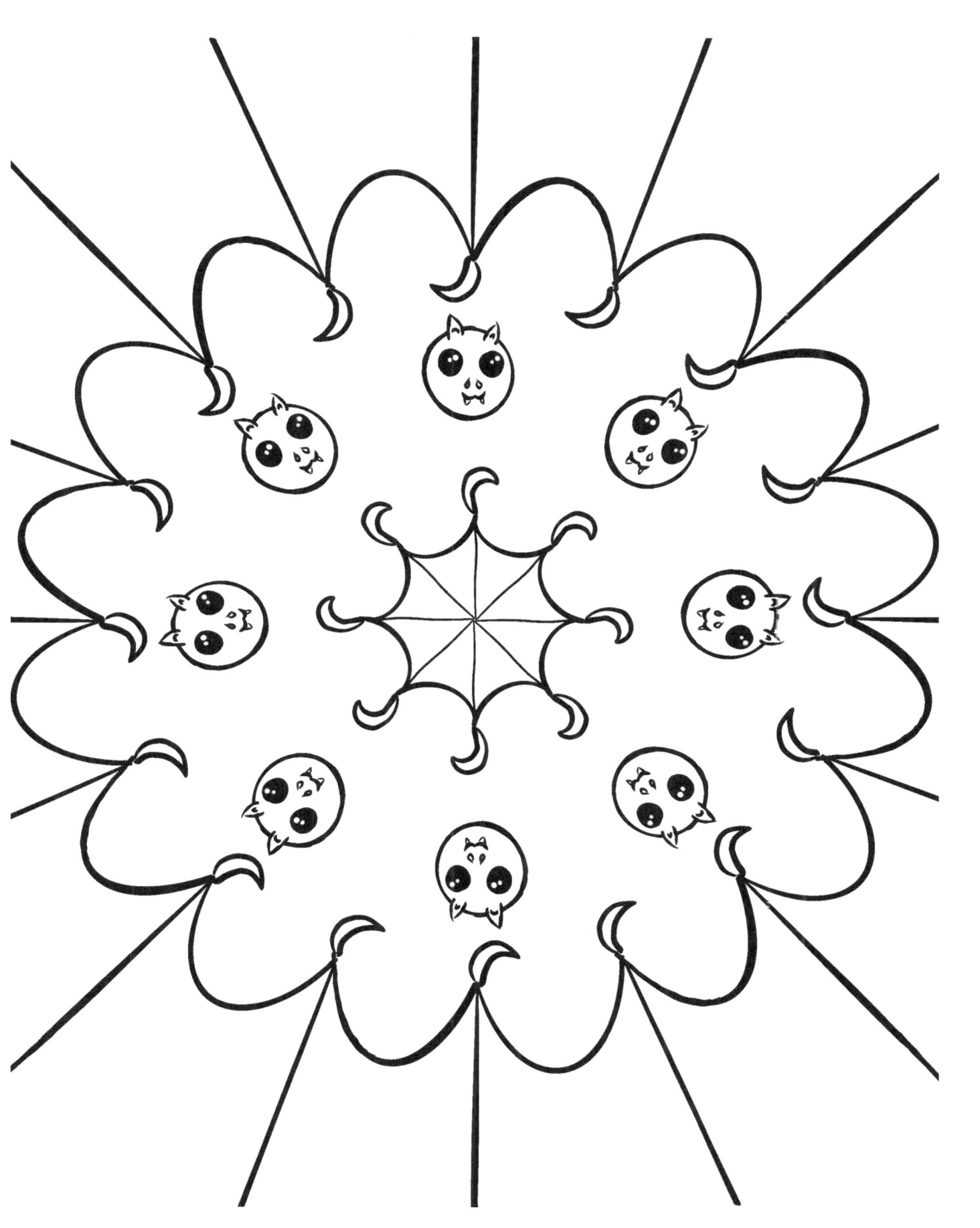

CASTLE HALLS

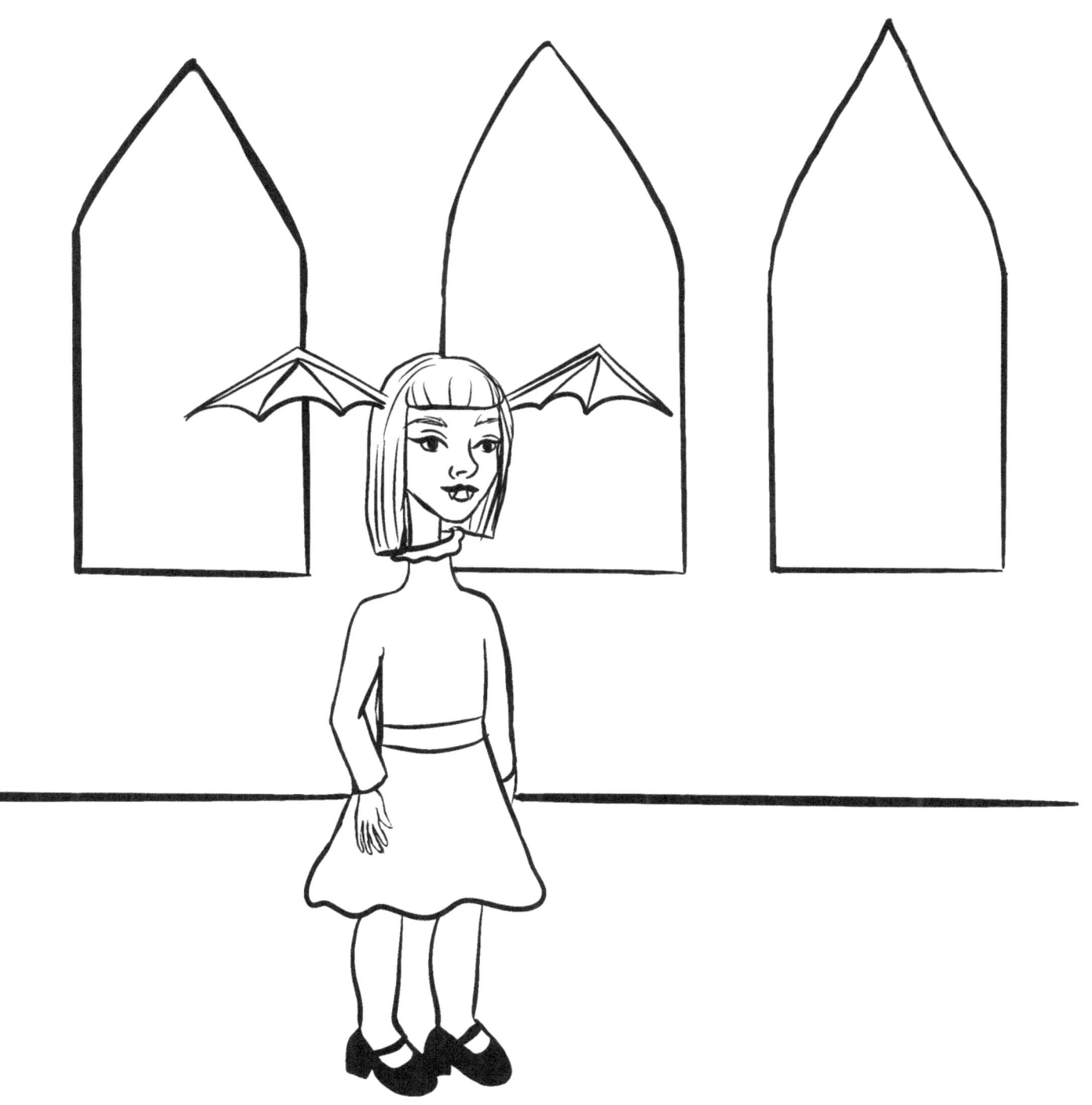

HEART WEBS

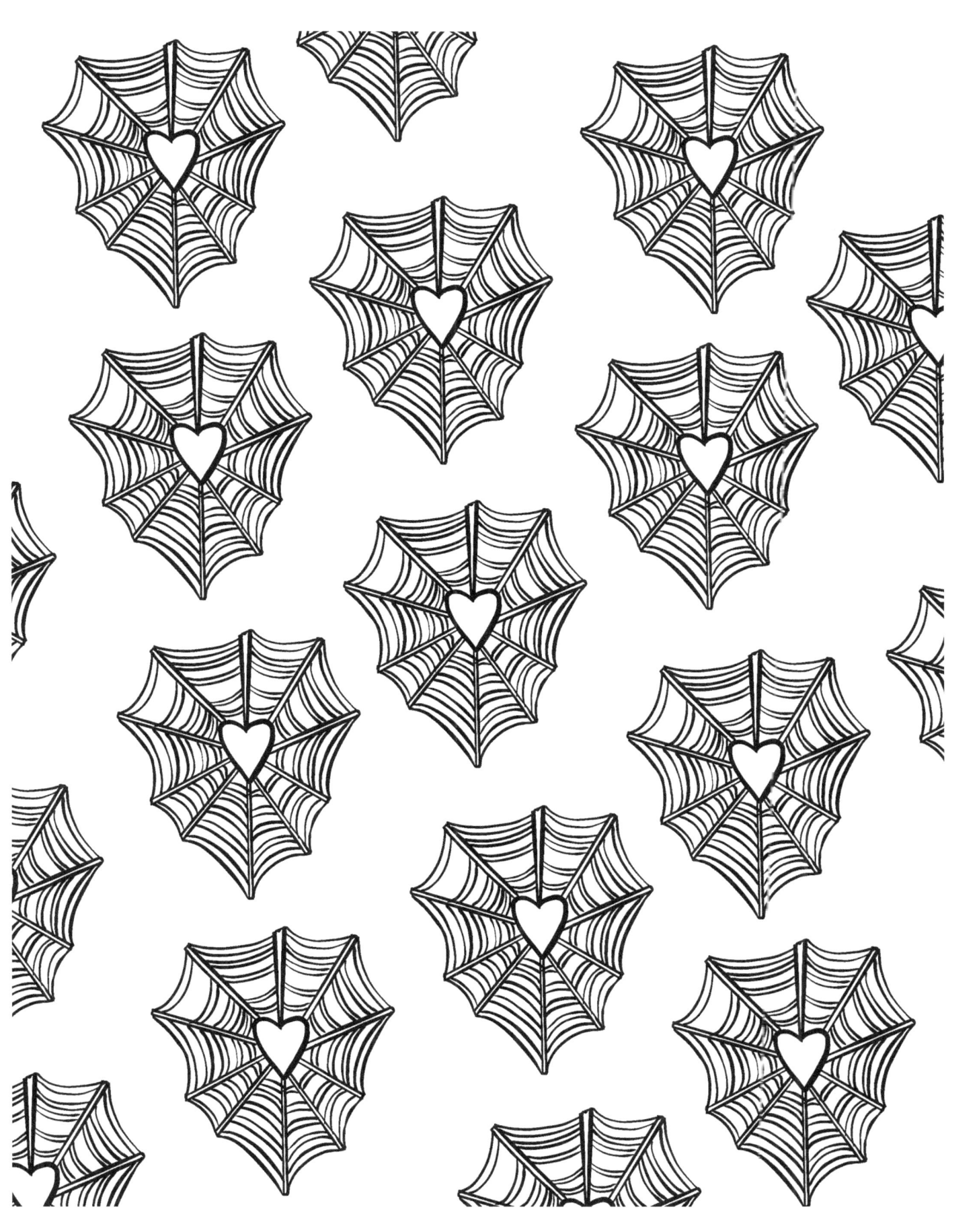

BABY BATS

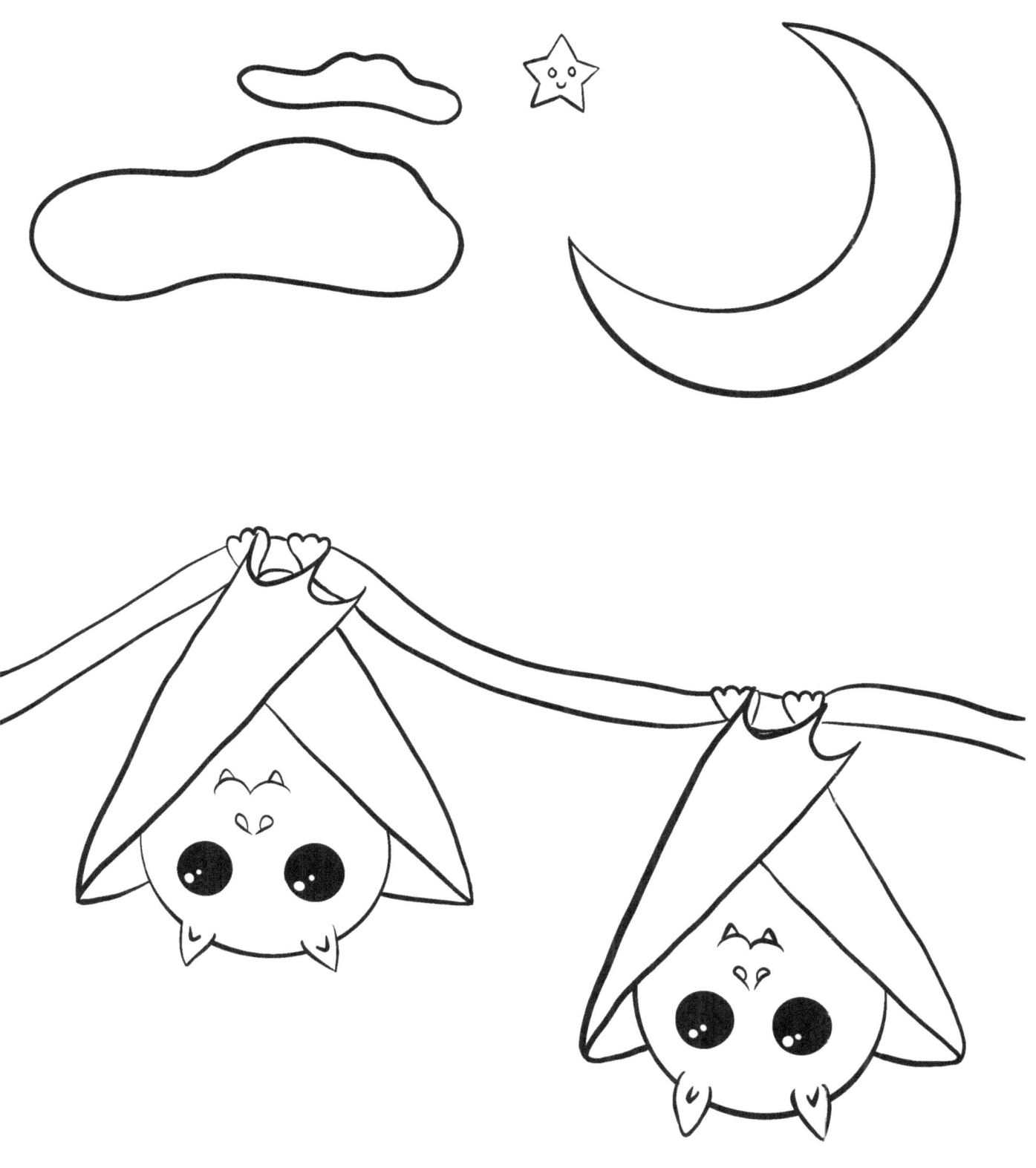

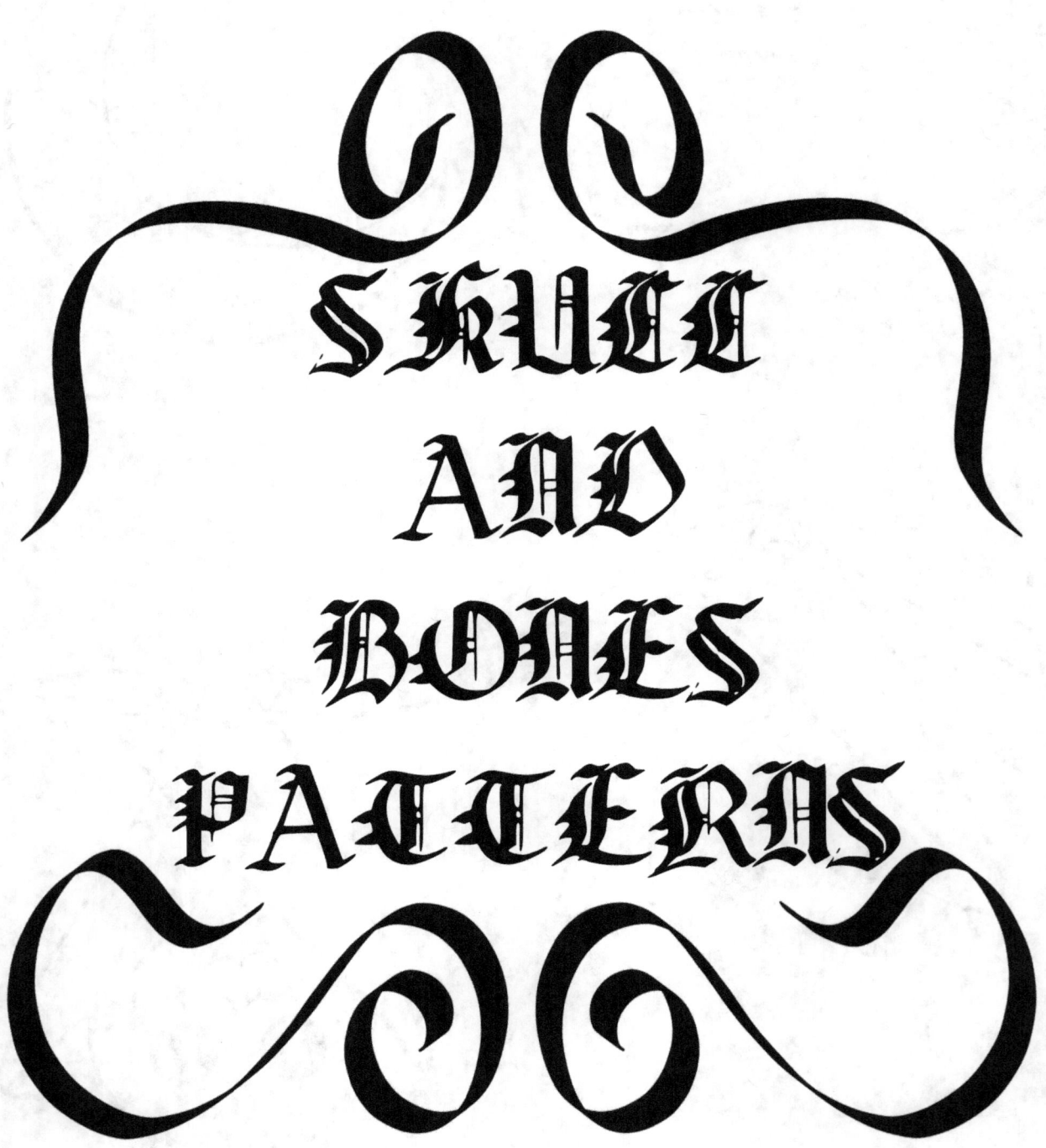

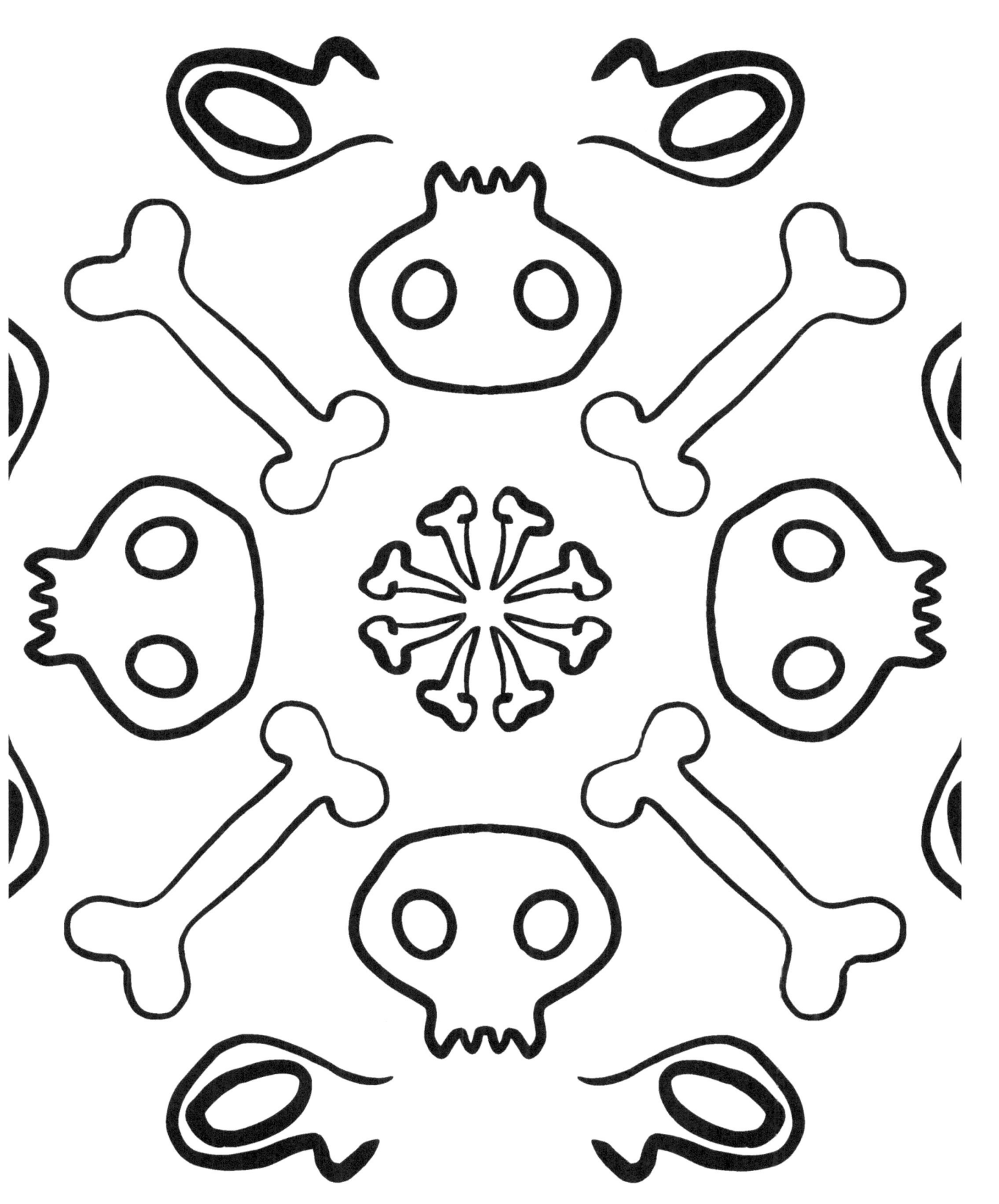

SPIDER WEB

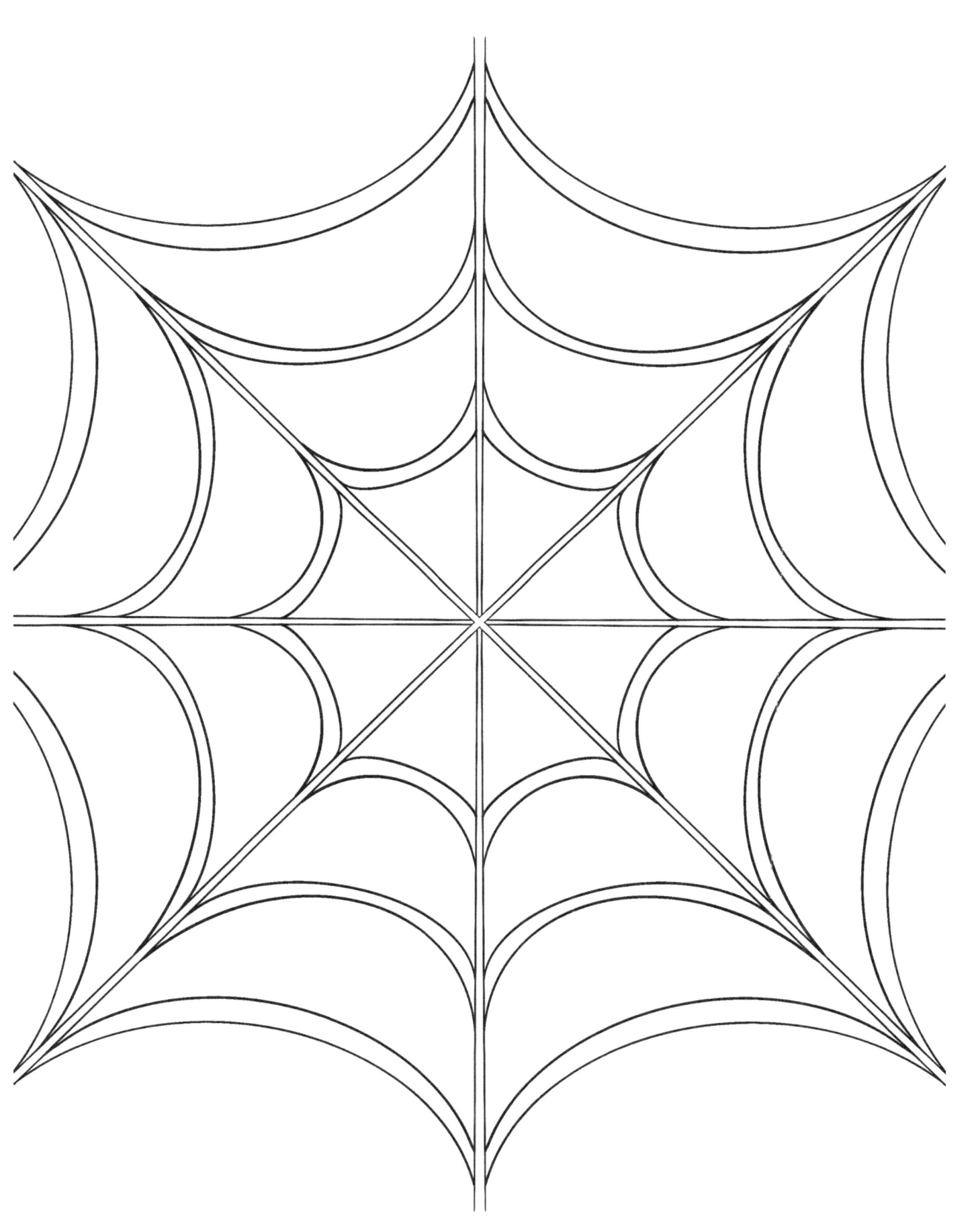

VAMPIRE STARS

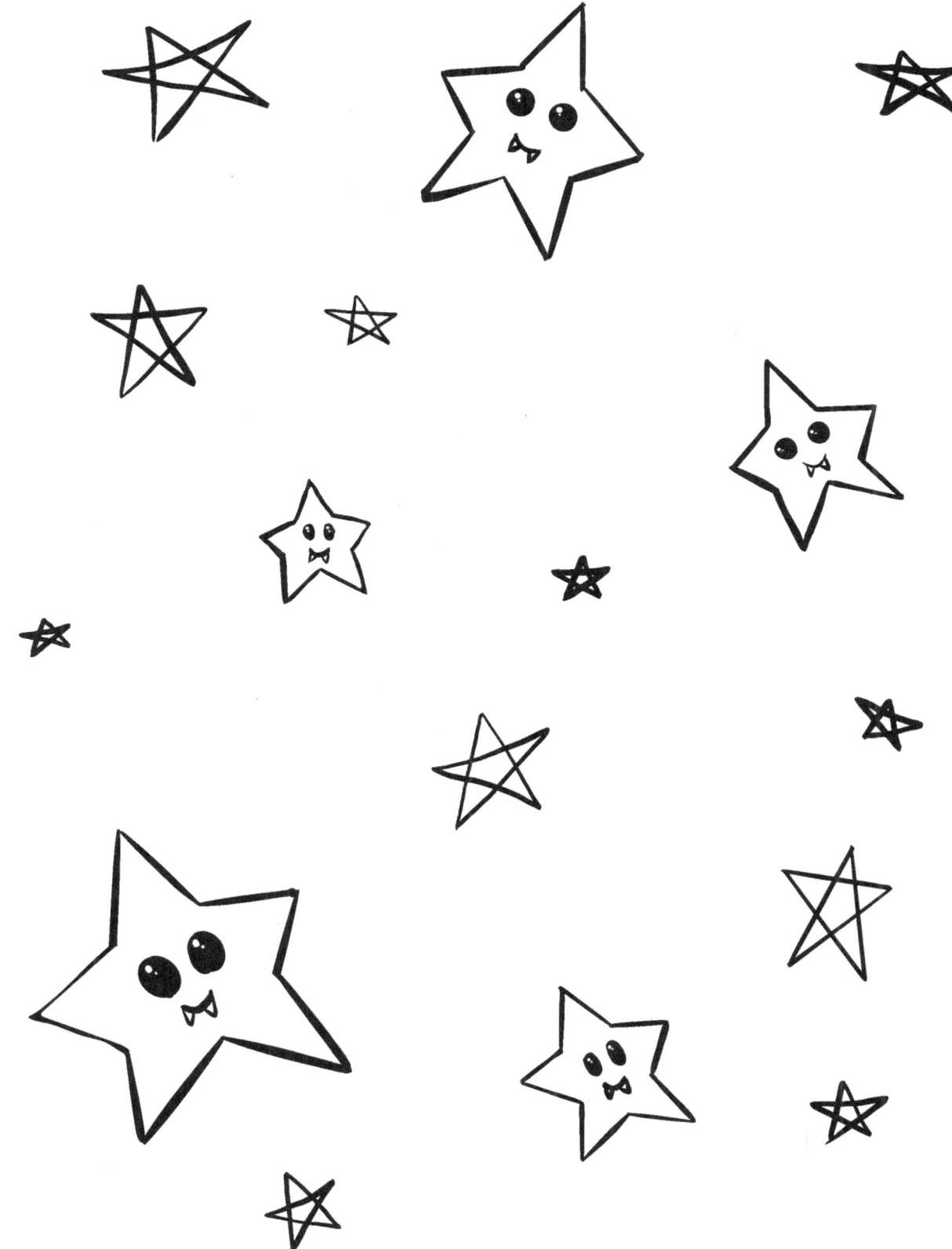

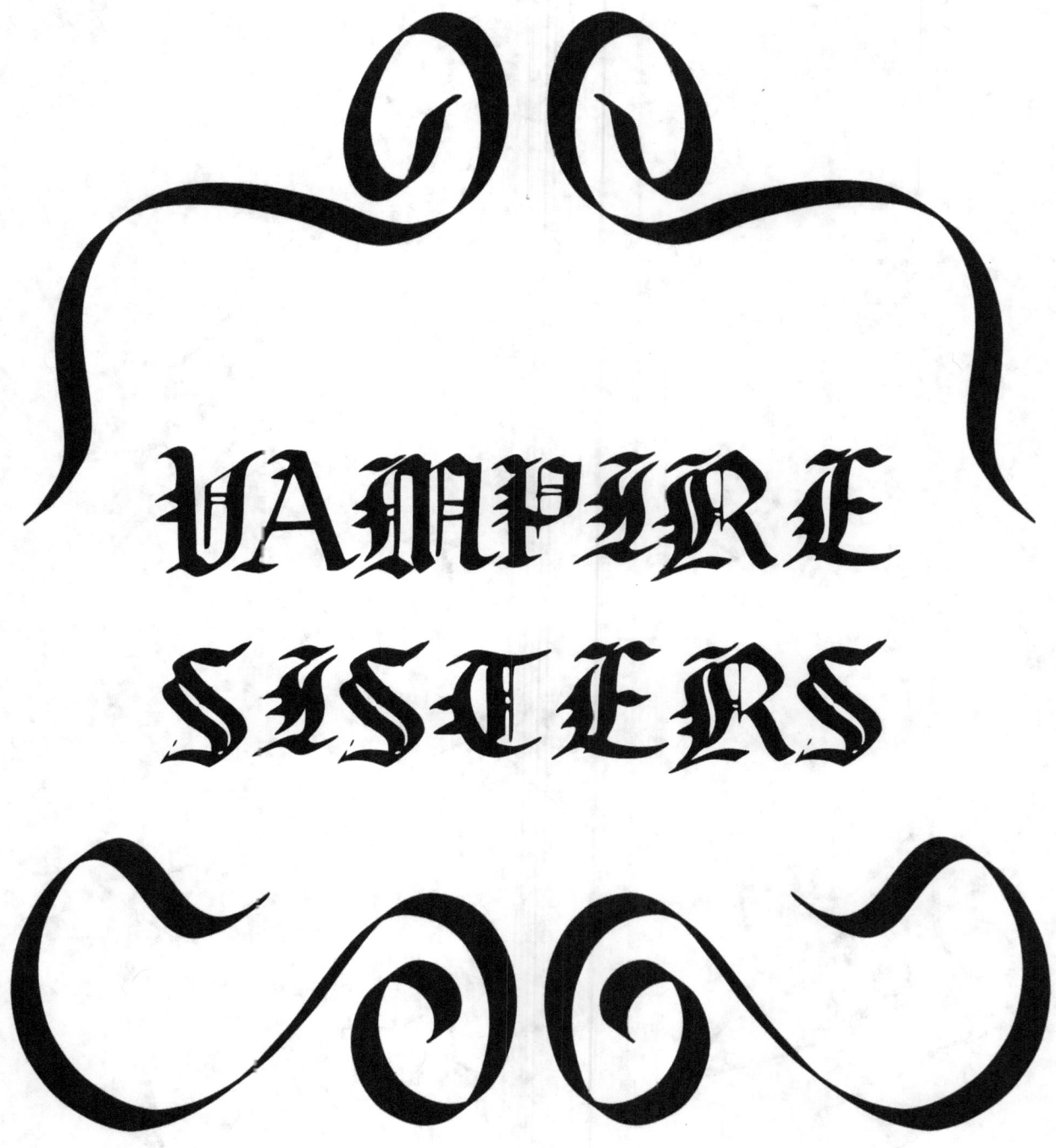

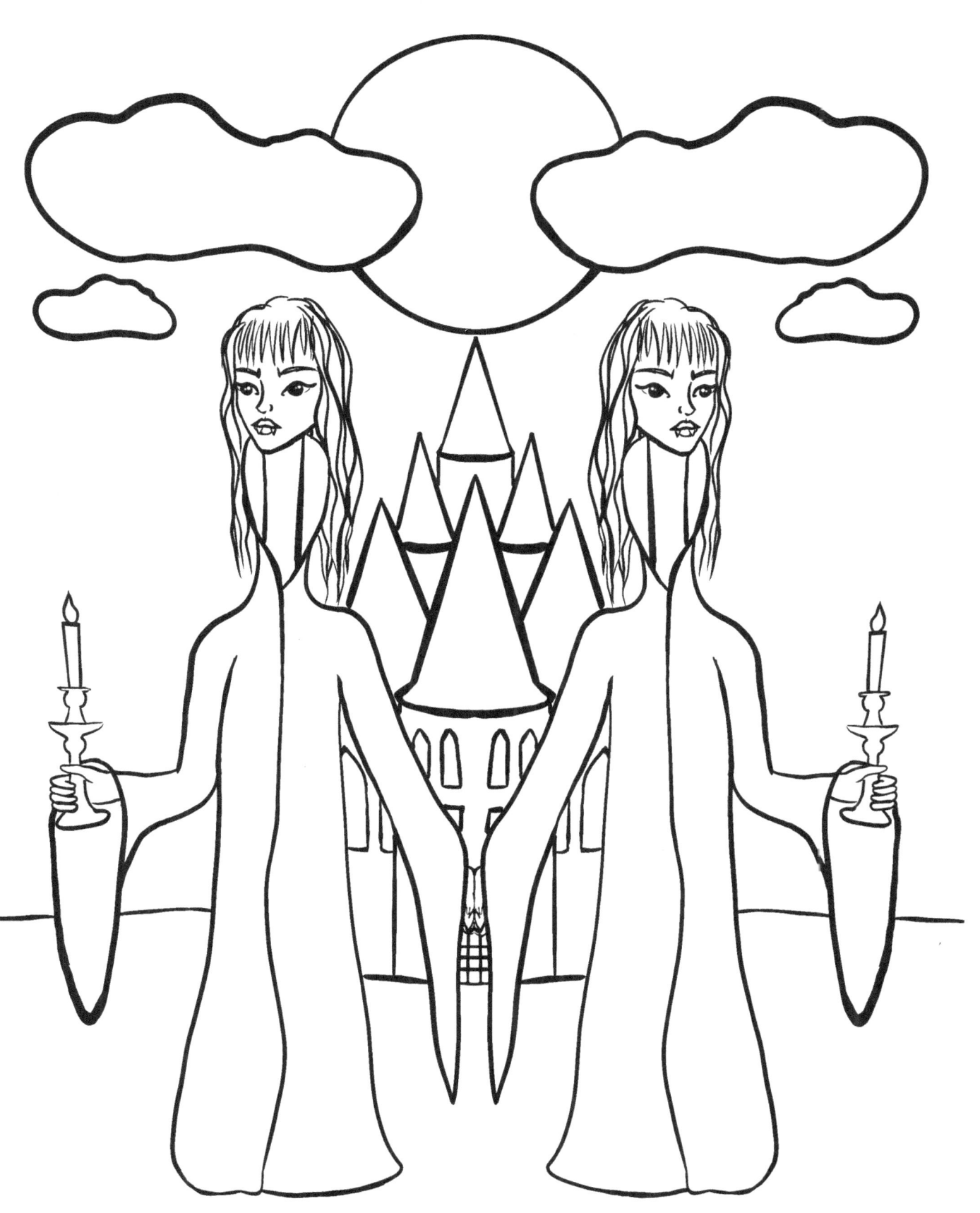

www.ingramcontent.com/pod-product-compliance
Lightning Source LLC
Chambersburg PA
CBHW082121220526
45472CB00009B/2256